D1497221

NATIONAL DRUG THREAT ASSESSMENT AND INTERNATIONAL DRUG CONTROL

DRUG TRANSIT AND DISTRIBUTION, INTERCEPTION AND CONTROL

Additional books in this series can be found on Nova's website
under the Series tab.

Additional E-books in this series can be found on Nova's website
under the E-book tab.

LAW, CRIME AND LAW ENFORCEMENT

Additional books in this series can be found on Nova's website
under the Series tab.

Additional E-books in this series can be found on Nova's website
under the E-book tab.

DRUG TRANSIT AND DISTRIBUTION, INTERCEPTION AND CONTROL

NATIONAL DRUG THREAT ASSESSMENT AND INTERNATIONAL DRUG CONTROL

PAUL ZIEGLER
EDITOR

Nova Science Publishers, Inc.
New York

NOTICE TO THE READER

The Publisher has taken reasonable care in the preparation of this book, but makes no expressed or implied warranty of any kind and assumes no responsibility for any errors or omissions. No liability is assumed for incidental or consequential damages in connection with or arising out of information contained in this book. The Publisher shall not be liable for any special, consequential, or exemplary damages resulting, in whole or in part, from the readers' use of, or reliance upon, this material. Any parts of this book based on government reports are so indicated and copyright is claimed for those parts to the extent applicable to compilations of such works.

Independent verification should be sought for any data, advice or recommendations contained in this book. In addition, no responsibility is assumed by the publisher for any injury and/or damage to persons or property arising from any methods, products, instructions, ideas or otherwise contained in this publication.

This publication is designed to provide accurate and authoritative information with regard to the subject matter covered herein. It is sold with the clear understanding that the Publisher is not engaged in rendering legal or any other professional services. If legal or any other expert assistance is required, the services of a competent person should be sought. FROM A DECLARATION OF PARTICIPANTS JOINTLY ADOPTED BY A COMMITTEE OF THE AMERICAN BAR ASSOCIATION AND A COMMITTEE OF PUBLISHERS.

Additional color graphics may be available in the e-book version of this book.

Library of Congress Cataloging-in-Publication Data
National drug threat assessment and international drug control / editor,
Paul Ziegler.
    p. cm.
 Includes index.
  ISBN 978-1-60876-065-7 (hbk.)
  1. Drug traffic--United States. 2. Drug traffic. 3. Drug
control--International cooperation. I. Ziegler, Paul, 1971-
HV5825.N3338 2011   363.45--dc23   2011024426

Published by Nova Science Publishers, Inc. † *New York*

CONTENTS

Preface   **vii**

Chapter 1   National Drug Threat Assessment - 2010   **1**
                 U.S. Department of Justice National Drug
                 Intelligence Center

Chapter 2   International Drug Control Policy   **89**
                 Liana Sun Wyler

Chapter Sources   **149**

Index   **151**

PREFACE

The global illegal drug trade represents a multi-dimensional challenge that has implications for U.S. national interests as well as the international community. According to the U.S. intelligence community, international drug trafficking can undermine political and regional stability and bolster the role and capabilities of organized crime in the drug trade. Key regions of concern include Latin American and Afghanistan, which are focal points in U.S. efforts to combat the production and transit of cocaine and heroin, respectively. Drug use and addiction have the potential to negatively affect the social fabric of communities, hinder economic development, and place an additional burden on national public health infrastructures. This book examines U.S. international drug control policy with a focus on the impact of drugs on society, drug trafficking organizations, and the global scope of the problem.

Chapter 1- Although drug use remained relatively stable from 2007 through 2008, more than 25 million individuals 12 years of age and older reported using an illicit drug or using a controlled prescription drug (CPD) nonmedically in 2008. Each year, drug-related deaths number in the thousands, and treatment admissions and emergency department (ED)visits both exceed a million. These and other consequences of drug abuse, including lost productivity associated with abuse, the impact on the criminal justice system, and the environmental impact that results from the production of illicit drugs, are estimated at nearly $215 billion annually.

Chapter 2- The global illegal drug trade represents a multi-dimensional challenge that has implications for U.S. national interests as well as the international community. Common illegal drugs trafficked internationally include cocaine, heroin, and methamphetamine. According to the U.S. intelligence community, international drug trafficking can undermine political and regional stability and bolster the role and capabilities of organized crime in the drug trade. Key regions of concern include Latin America and Afghanistan, which are focal points in U.S. efforts to combat the production and transit of cocaine and heroin, respectively. Drug use and addiction have the potential to negatively affect the social fabric of communities, hinder economic development, and place an additional burden on national public health infrastructures.

In: National Drug Threat Assessment ...   ISBN: 978-1-60876-065-7
Editor: Paul Ziegler   © 2011 Nova Science Publishers, Inc.

Chapter 1

NATIONAL DRUG THREAT ASSESSMENT - 2010

United States Department of Justice
National Drug Intelligence Center

EXECUTIVE SUMMARY

Overall, the availability of illicit drugs in the United States is increasing.[1] In fact, in 2009 the prevalence of four of the five major drugs—heroin, methamphetamine, marijuana, and MDMA (3,4- methylenedioxy-methamphetamine)—was widespread and increasing in some areas. Conversely, cocaine shortages first identified in 2007 persisted in many markets. Significant trends include:

- Increased heroin availability evidenced by higher purity, lower prices, and elevated numbers of heroin-related overdoses and overdose deaths is partly attributable to increased production in Mexico from 17 pure metric tons in 2007 to 38 pure metric tons in 2008, according to U.S. Government estimates.
- Despite recent government of Mexico (GOM) efforts to prohibit the importation of methamphetamine precursor chemicals, methamphetamine availability increased as the result of higher production in Mexico using alternative, less-efficient precursors.

Sustained domestic production also contributed to the increased availability levels.

- Marijuana production increased in Mexico, resulting in increased flow of the drug across the Southwest Border, including through the Tohono O'odham Reservation in Arizona.
- Asian drug trafficking organizations (DTOs) are responsible for the resurgence in MDMA availability in the United States, particularly since 2005. These groups produce the drug in Canada and smuggle it across the Northern Border into the United States.
- Cocaine shortages have persisted in many U.S. drug markets since early 2007, primarily because of decreased cocaine production in Colombia but also because of increased worldwide demand for cocaine, especially in Europe; high cocaine seizure levels that continued through 2009; and enhanced GOM counterdrug efforts. These factors most likely resulted in decreased amounts of cocaine being transported from Colombia to the U.S.–Mexico border for subsequent smuggling into the United States.

Although drug use remained relatively stable from 2007 through 2008, more than 25 million individuals 12 years of age[2] and older reported using an illicit drug or using a controlled prescription drug (CPD) nonmedically in 2008. Each year, drug-related deaths number in the thousands, and treatment admissions and emergency department (ED)visits both exceed a million. These and other consequences of drug abuse, including lost productivity associated with abuse, the impact on the criminal justice system, and the environmental impact that results from the production of illicit drugs, are estimated at nearly $215 billion[3] annually.

Mexican DTOs continue to represent the single greatest drug trafficking threat to the United States. Mexican DTOs, already the predominant wholesale suppliers of illicit drugs in the United States, are gaining even greater strength in eastern drug markets where Colombian DTO strength is diminishing. The extent of Mexican DTO influence over domestic drug trafficking was evidenced in several ways in 2009. For example:

- Mexican DTOs were the only DTOs operating in every region of the country.
- Mexican DTOs increased their cooperation with U.S.-based street and prison gangs to distribute drugs. In many areas, these gangs were using their alliances with Mexican DTOs to facilitate an expansion of

their midlevel and retail drug distribution operations into more rural and suburban areas.

- In 2009, midlevel and retail drug distribution in the United States was dominated by more than 900,000 criminally active gang members representing approximately 20,000 street gangs in more than 2,500 cities.
- Mexican DTOs increased the flow of several drugs (heroin, methamphetamine, and marijuana) into the United States, primarily because they increased production of those drugs in Mexico.
- Drugs smuggled into the United States by Mexican DTOs usually are transported in private or commercial vehicles; however, Mexican DTOs also use cross-border tunnels, subterranean passageways, and low- flying small or ultralight aircraft to move drugs from Mexico into the United States.
- Mexican DTOs smuggled bulk cash drug proceeds totaling tens of billions of dollars from the United States through the Southwest Border and into Mexico. Much of the bulk cash (millions each week) was consolidated by the DTOs in several key areas, including Atlanta, Chicago, Los Angeles, New York City, and North Carolina, where it was prepared for transport to the U.S.–Mexico border and then smuggled into Mexico.
- According to the Bureau of Alcohol, Tobacco, Firearms and Explosives (ATF), Mexican DTO members or associates acquire thousands of weapons each year in Arizona, California, and Texas and smuggle them across the border to Mexico.

The threat posed by the diversion and abuse of CPDs, primarily pain relievers, is increasing, evidenced by the sharp rise in the percentage (4.6% in 2007 to 9.8% in 2009) of state and local law enforcement agencies reporting CPDs as the greatest drug threat in their area.

- Increased abuse of CPDs has led to elevated numbers of deaths related to prescription opioids, which increased 98 percent from 2002 to 2006.
- Unscrupulous physicians who operate purported pain clinics in Florida—which until recently did not have a Prescription Drug Monitoring Program (PDMP)—are a significant source of supply for prescription opioids distributed in numerous states.

National Drug Intelligence Center (NDIC) analysts estimate that the overall threat posed by illicit drugs will not diminish in the near term. Although NDIC believes that sustained shortages of cocaine will persist in some U.S. markets in 2010, the availability of heroin, methamphetamine, and marijuana will increase, largely the result of increased production of the drugs in Mexico. The growing strength and organization of criminal gangs, including their alliances with large Mexican DTOs, will make disrupting illicit drug availability and distribution increasingly difficult for law enforcement agencies. The increased enforcement against illegal pain clinics and the growing number of PDMPs will disrupt the supply of CPDs to prescription opioid users in some areas, with the result that some users will seek opioids from other sources and some will switch to heroin.

IMPACT OF DRUGS ON SOCIETY

The trafficking and abuse of drugs in the United States affect nearly all aspects of our lives. The economic cost alone is immense, estimated at nearly $215 billion. The damage caused by drug abuse and addiction is reflected in an overburdened justice system, a strained healthcare system, lost productivity, and environmental destruction.

The Demand for Illicit Drugs

NSDUH data show that in 2008, 14.2 percent of individuals 12 years of age and older had used illicit drugs during the past year. Marijuana is the most commonly used illicit drug, with 25.8 million individuals 12 years of age and older (10.3%) reporting past year use. That rate remains stable from the previous year (10.1%) (see Table B 1 in Appendix B). Psychotherapeutics[4] ranked second, with 15.2 million individuals reporting past year "nonmedical use" in 2008, a decrease from 16.3 million in 2007. In 2008, approximately 5.3 million individuals aged 12 and older reported past year cocaine use, 850,000 reported past year methamphetamine use, and 453,000 reported past year heroin use.

Rates of drug use vary by age. Rates are highest for young adults aged 18 to 25, with 33.5 percent reporting illicit drug use in the past year. Nineteen percent of youth aged 12 to 17 report past year illicit drug use. Finally, 10.3

percent of adults aged 26 and older report past year illicit drug use. These rates are relatively stable when compared with 2007 rates.

In 2008, approximately 2.9 million individuals tried an illicit drug or used a prescription drug nonmedically for the first time, representing nearly 8,000 initiates per day. More than half of these new users (56.6%) report that marijuana was the first illicit substance that they had tried. Other past year illicit drug initiates report that their first drug was a psychotherapeutic drug used nonmedically (29.6%), an inhalant (9.7%), or a hallucinogen (3.2%). By drug category, marijuana and pain relievers used nonmedically each had an estimated 2.2 million past year first-time users. Also identified frequently as the first drug used by initiates were tranquilizers (nonmedical use—1.1 million), ecstasy/MDMA (0.9 million), inhalants (0.7 million), cocaine (0.7 million), and stimulants (0.6 million). Methamphetamine appears to be fading in popularity among initiates. In 2008, an estimated 95,000 individuals tried methamphetamine for the first time—a 39 percent decrease from the 2007 estimate (157,000) and a 70 percent decrease from the 2004 estimate (318,000).

The Consequences of Illicit Drug Use

The consequences of illicit drug use are widespread, causing permanent physical and emotional damage to users and negatively impacting their families, coworkers, and many others with whom they have contact. Drug use negatively impacts a user's health, often leading to sickness and disease. In many cases, users die prematurely from drug overdoses or other drug-associated illnesses (see text box on page 4). Some users are parents, whose deaths leave their children in the care of relatives or in foster care. Drug law violations constitute a substantial proportion of incarcerations in local, state, and federal facilities and represent the most common arrest category.

COLOMBIAN COCAINE PRODUCERS INCREASE USE OF A HARMFUL CUTTING AGENT

Since late 2007, cocaine has increasingly contained levamisole, a pharmaceutical agent that typically is used for livestock deworming. According to Drug Enforcement Administration (DEA) Cocaine Signature Program data, before 2008, less than 10 percent of the tested wholesale-level cocaine samples contained levamisole. By 2009, approximately 71 percent of the tested cocaine samples contained levamisole. Because levamisole is being found in kilogram quantities of cocaine, investigators are confident that Colombian traffickers are adding it as part of the production process, possibly to enhance the effects of the cocaine. However, levamisole can be hazardous to humans, especially those with weakened immune systems. Ingesting levamisole can cause a person to develop agranulocytosis, a serious, sometimes fatal, blood disorder. At least 20 confirmed and probable cases of agranulocytosis, including two deaths, have been associated with cocaine adulterated with levamisole. The consequences of abusing levamisole are serious enough that in September 2009, the Substance Abuse and Mental Health Services Administration (SAMHSA) issued a nationwide public alert on its effects.

Impact on Health and Health Care Systems

Drug use and abuse may lead to specialized treatment, ED visits (sometimes involving death), contraction of illnesses, and prolonged hospital stays.

In 2008, NSDUH estimated that 7 million individuals aged 12 and older were dependent on or had abused illicit drugs in the past year, compared with 6.9 million in 2007. The drugs with the highest dependence or abuse levels were marijuana, prescription pain relievers, and cocaine. The number of individuals reporting past year marijuana abuse or dependence was 4.2 million in 2008, compared with 3.9 million in 2007; the number of individuals reporting past year prescription pain reliever abuse or dependence was 1.7 million in both 2007 and 2008; and the number of individuals reporting past year cocaine abuse or dependence was 1.4 million in 2008, compared with 1.6 million in 2007.

Many individuals who become dependent on illicit drugs eventually seek treatment. The Treatment Episode Data Set (TEDS) provides information regarding the demographics and substance abuse patterns of treatment admissions to state-licensed treatment facilities for drug dependence. In 2007, there were approximately 1.8 million admissions to state-licensed treatment facilities for illicit drug dependence or abuse. The highest percentage of admissions reported opiates as the primary drug of choice (31%, primarily heroin) followed by marijuana/ hashish (27%), cocaine (22%), and stimulants (13%). Although approaches to treatment vary by drug, more than half of the admissions were to ambulatory (outpatient, intensive outpatient, and detox) facilities rather than residential facilities. (See Table B2 in Appendix B for data on admissions for specific drugs.)

Individuals often experience adverse reactions to drugs—including nonfatal overdoses—that require them to go to the hospital. In 2006, the Drug Abuse Warning Network (DAWN) reported that of 113 million hospital ED visits—1,742,887 (1.5%)—were related to drug misuse or drug abuse. An estimated 31 percent of these visits involved illicit drugs only, 28 percent involved CPDs, and 13 percent involved illicit drugs in combination with alcohol. When drug misuse or abuse plays a role in these ED visits, the most commonly reported substances are cocaine, marijuana, heroin, and stimulants (typically amphetamines or methamphetamine).

A 2007 DAWN survey of 63 metropolitan areas found an average of 12.1 deaths per 100,000 persons related to drug use.[5] Rates of drug-related deaths range from 1.1 per 100,000 in Sioux Falls, South Dakota, to 26.1 per 100,000 in the New Orleans area. DAWN also records the number of drug-related suicide deaths. In 2007, the number of drug-related suicides per 100,000 persons ranged from less than one in several jurisdictions (including Chicago, Dallas-Fort Worth, and Minneapolis) to 6.2 per 100,000 in Fargo, North Dakota. To put these statistics in perspective, the Centers for Disease Control and Prevention (CDC) reports other nonnatural death rates as follows: Motor vehicle accidents, 15.1 per 100,000; nontransport accidents (e.g., falls, accidental drownings), 24.4 per 100,000; suicide, 11.1 per 100,000; and homicides, 6.2 per 100,000.

The consequences of drug use usually are not limited to the user and often extend to the user's family and the greater community. According to SAMHSA, combined data from 2002 to 2007 indicate that during the prior year, an estimated 2.1 million American children (3%) lived with at least one parent who was dependent on or abused illicit drugs, and 1 in 10 children under 18 lived with a substance-addicted or substance-abusing parent.[6] Moreover, the U.S. Department of Health and Human Services estimated in 1999 that substance abuse was a factor in two-thirds of all foster care placements.

Many states have enacted drug-endangered children laws to protect children from the consequences of drug production, trafficking, and abuse. Typically associated with methamphetamine production, drug-endangered children are exposed not only to abuse and neglect but also to fires, explosions, and physical health hazards such as toxic chemicals. In 2009, 980 children were reported to the El Paso Intelligence Center (EPIC) as present at or affected by methamphetamine laboratories, including 8 who were injured and 2 who were killed at the laboratories. These statistics do not include children killed by random gunfire associated with drug activity or who were physically or sexually abused by a "caretaker" involved in drug trafficking or under the influence of drugs.

Impact on Crime and Criminal Justice Systems

The consequences of illicit drug use impact the entire criminal justice system, taxing resources at each stage of the arrest, adjudication, incarceration, and post-release supervision process. Although drug courts and diversion programs in many jurisdictions have helped to alleviate this burden (see text box on page 6), substance abuse within the criminal justice population remains widespread.

The most recent annual data from the Federal Bureau of Investigation (FBI) show that 12.2 percent of more than 14 million arrests in 2008 were for drug violations, the most common arrest crime category. The proportion of total drug arrests has increased over the past 20 years: in 1987, only 7.4 percent of all arrests were for drug violations. Approximately 4 percent of all homicides in 2008 were drug- related, a percentage that has not changed significantly over the same 20-year period.

The characteristics of populations under correctional supervision reflect these arrest patterns. According to the Bureau of Justice Statistics (BJS), 20 percent of state prisoners and 53 percent of federal prisoners are incarcerated because of a drug offense. Moreover, 27 percent of individuals on probation and 37 percent of individuals on parole at the end of 2007 had committed a drug offense.

DRUG COURTS

To alleviate the burden that drug use and abuse have caused to the nation's criminal justice system, most jurisdictions have developed drug courts or other diversion programs aimed at breaking the drug addiction and crime cycle. In these nonadversarial, coordinated approaches to processing drug cases, participants receive a full continuum of treatment services, are subject to frequent urinalyses, and experience strict judicial monitoring in lieu of traditional incarceration. Once the offender successfully completes treatment, charges may be dropped.

Since the first drug court became operational in Miami in 1989, the number of drug courts has grown each year, and such courts now exist in all 50 states as well as the District of Columbia, Northern Mariana Islands, Puerto Rico, and Indian Country. As of July 2009, there were 2,038 active drug court programs and 226 in the planning stages. Research has shown that drug courts are associated with reduced recidivism by participants and result in cost savings. For instance, a 2006 study of nine California drug courts showed that drug court graduates had recidivism rates of 17 percent, while a comparison group who did not participate in drug court had recidivism rates of 41 percent. A study of the drug court in Portland, Oregon, found that the program reduced crime by 30 percent over 5 years and saved the county more than $79 million over 10 years. With success stories abundant, drug courts have gained approval at the local, state, and federal levels.

The drug-crime link is also reflected in arrestee data. In 2008, the Arrestee Drug Abuse Monitoring (ADAM) II program found that the median percentage of male arrestees who tested positive in the 10 ADAM II cities for any of 10 drugs, including cocaine, marijuana, methamphetamine, opioids, and phencyclidine (PCP), was 67.6 percent, down slightly from 69.2 percent in 2007. Other data reflect the link as well. In 2002, a BJS survey found that 68 percent of jail inmates were dependent on or abusing drugs and alcohol and that 55 percent had used illicit drugs during the month before their offense. In 2004, a similar BJS self-report survey identified the drug-crime link more precisely: 17 percent of state prisoners and 18 percent of federal prisoners had committed their most recent offense to acquire money to buy drugs. Property and drug offenders were more likely than violent and public-order offenders to commit crimes for drug money.

Impact on Productivity

Premature mortality, illness, injury leading to incapacitation, and imprisonment all serve to directly reduce national productivity. Public financial resources expended in the areas of health care and criminal justice as a result of illegal drug trafficking and use are resources that would otherwise be available for other policy initiatives.

There is a great loss of productivity associated with drug-related premature mortality. In 2005, 26,858 deaths were unintentional or undetermined-intent poisonings; in 2004, 95 percent of these poisonings were caused by drugs. Although it is difficult to place a dollar value on a human life, a rough calculation of lost productivity can be made based on the present discounted value of a person's lifetime earnings.

There are also health-related productivity losses. An individual who enters a residential drug treatment program or is admitted to a hospital for drug treatment becomes incapacitated and is removed from the labor force. According to TEDS data, there were approximately 1.8 million admissions to state-licensed treatment facilities for illicit drug dependence or abuse in 2007. Productivity losses in this area alone are enormous. Health-related productivity losses are higher still when lost productivity associated with drug-related hospital admissions (including victims of drug-related crimes) is included.

The approximately one-quarter of offenders in state and local correctional facilities and the more than half of offenders in federal facilities incarcerated on drug-related charges represent an estimated 620,000 individuals who are not in the workforce. The cost of their incarceration therefore has two components: keeping them behind bars and the results of their non-productivity while they are there.

Finally, there is productivity lost to drug- related unemployment and drug-related absenteeism. According to the 2008 NSDUH, 19.6 percent of unemployed adults may be defined as current users of illicit drugs. Based on population estimates from the same study, this translates into approximately 1.8 million unemployed individuals who were current drug abusers. Further, approximately 8 percent of individuals employed full time and 10.2 percent of individuals employed part-time were current users of illicit drugs. Individuals who are employed but have chronic absenteeism resulting from illicit drug use also accrue substantial lost productivity.

Impact on the Environment

The environmental impact of illicit drugs is largely the result of outdoor cannabis cultivation and methamphetamine production. Many of the chemicals used to produce methamphetamine are flammable, and the improper storage, use, and disposal of such chemicals that are typical among methamphetamine producers often lead to fires and explosions at clandestine laboratories. Additionally, the process used to produce methamphetamine results in toxic chemicals—between 5 and 7 pounds of waste per pound of methamphetamine—that are typically discarded improperly in fields, streams, forests, and sewer systems, causing extensive environmental damage.

Currently, there are no conclusive estimates regarding the nationwide cost of methamphetamine production site remediation because many of the methamphetamine laboratories and dumpsites in the United States are undiscovered due to their clandestine locations. However, in California alone, from January through December 10, 2009, the California Department of Toxic Substance Control responded to and cleaned up 232 laboratories and dumpsites at a cost of $776,889, or approximately $3,349 per site.

Outdoor cannabis cultivation, particularly on public lands, is causing increasing environmental damage. Grow site operators often contaminate and alter watersheds, clear-cut native vegetation, discard garbage and non-biodegradable materials at deserted sites, create wildfire hazards, and divert natural water courses. For example, cultivators often dam streams and redirect the water through plastic gravity-fed irrigation tubing to supply water to individual plants. The high demand for water often strains small streams and damages downstream vegetation that depend on consistent water flow. In addition, law enforcement officials are increasingly encountering dumpsites of highly toxic insecticides, chemical repellants, and poisons that are produced in Mexico, purchased by Mexican criminal groups, and transported into the country for use at their cannabis grow sites. These toxic chemicals enter and contaminate ground water, pollute watersheds, kill fish and other wildlife, and eventually enter residential water supplies. Moreover, the National Parks Conservation Association (NPCA) reports that while preparing land for cannabis cultivation, growers commonly clear the forest understory, which allows nonnative plants to supplant native ones, adversely affecting the ecosystem. They also terrace the land—especially in mountainous areas—which results in rapid erosion.

Limited research on the environmental impact of the improper disposal of pharmaceuticals[7] indicates that contamination from dissolved pharmaceutical drugs is present in extremely low levels in most of the nation's water supply. The harm to aquatic life and the environment has not been determined, and according to the Environmental Protection Agency, scientists have found no evidence of adverse human health effects from the minute residue found in water supplies. Nonetheless, as a precaution based on environmental research to date, the ONDCP and the Food and Drug Administration suggest that consumers use take-back programs to dispose of unused prescription drugs (see text box on page 52 in Vulnerabilities section).

DRUG TRAFFICKING ORGANIZATIONS

Wholesale-level DTOs, especially Mexican DTOs, constitute the greatest drug trafficking threat to the United States. These organizations derive tens of billions of dollars annually from the trafficking and abuse of illicit drugs and associated activities. All of the adverse societal impact resulting from the illicit drug trade begins with the criminal acts of DTOs that produce, transport, and distribute the drugs.

The influence of Mexican DTOs, already the dominant wholesale drug traffickers in the United States, is still expanding, primarily in areas where the direct influence of Colombian DTOs is diminishing.

Mexican DTOs are more deeply entrenched in drug trafficking activities in the United States than any other DTOs. They are the only DTOs that are operating in all nine Organized Crime Drug Enforcement Task Force (OCDETF) regions (see Map A1 in Appendix A) and all 32 High Intensity Drug Trafficking Areas (HIDTAs) (see Map A2 in Appendix A). They are active in more cities throughout the country than any other DTOs. Law enforcement reporting and case initiation data show that Mexican DTOs control most of the wholesale cocaine, heroin, and methamphetamine distribution in the United States as well as much of the marijuana distribution (see Table B3 in Appendix B).

In the past few years, Mexican DTOs expanded their operations in the Florida/Caribbean, Mid-Atlantic, New York/New Jersey, and New England Regions, where, in the past, Colombian DTOs were the leading suppliers of cocaine and heroin. As a result, the direct influence of Colombian DTOs has diminished further, although they remain a source for wholesale quantities of cocaine and heroin in many eastern states, especially New York and New Jersey. Mexican DTOs have expanded their presence by increasing their transportation and distribution networks, directly supplying Dominican drug distributors that had previously distributed cocaine and heroin provided primarily by Colombian DTOs. The switch by Dominican DTOs from Colombian to Mexican suppliers is most evident in the Mid-Atlantic Region, specifically in the Philadelphia/Camden and Washington/Baltimore areas. In these locations, some Dominican DTOs bypass Colombian sources of supply in New York City and Miami and obtain cocaine and heroin directly from Mexican sources or from sources in the Caribbean or in South America.

The supply arrangement between Mexican and Dominican DTOs has aided Dominican DTOs and criminal groups in expanding their midlevel and retail drug distribution networks, primarily in the Mid-Atlantic Region, but also in other regions such as the Great Lakes and Southwest. The establishment of multiple sources of supply—rather than reliance entirely on Colombian sources—has also enabled Dominican DTOs to lower costs and increase profit margins.

The direct effect of the Mexican DTO expansion in eastern states on the drug trafficking activities of Italian Organized Crime (IOC) groups is unclear, although IOC drug trafficking appeared to diminish in 2009 as Mexican DTO influence increased. In 2008, drug trafficking by IOC in eastern states appeared to be increasing, based on information revealed through several significant multiagency drug investigations. However, in 2009, there were no similar drug cases involving IOC, and the relative strength of these groups in drug trafficking in eastern states now is unclear.

DRUG CARTELS, DRUG TRAFFICKING ORGANIZATIONS, CRIMINAL GROUPS, AND GANGS

Drug cartels are large, highly sophisticated organizations composed of multiple DTOs and cells with specific assignments such as drug transportation, security/enforcement, or money laundering. Drug cartel command-and-control structures are based outside the United States; however, they produce, transport, and distribute illicit drugs domestically with the assistance of DTOs that are either a part of or in an alliance with the cartel.

Drug trafficking organizations (DTOs) are complex organizations with highly defined command-and-control structures that produce, transport, and distribute large quantities of one or more illicit drugs.

Criminal groups operating in the United States are numerous and range from small to moderately sized, loosely knit groups that distribute one or more drugs at the retail level and midlevel.

Street gangs are defined by the National Alliance of Gang Investigators' Associations as groups or associations of three or more persons with a common identifying sign, symbol, or name, the members of which individually or collectively engage in criminal activity that creates an atmosphere of fear and intimidation.

Prison gangs are highly structured criminal networks that operate within the federal and state prison system and in local communities through members who have been released from prison.

Outlaw motorcycle gangs (OMGs) are highly structured criminal organizations whose members engage in criminal activities such as violent crimes, weapons trafficking, and drug trafficking. OMGs maintain a strong centralized leadership that implements rules regulating membership, conduct, and criminal activity.

Asian DTOs have expanded their influence nationally in recent years by trafficking MDMA and high-potency marijuana— drugs that do not put them in direct competition with Mexican, Colombian, or Dominican DTOs.

The rising influence of Asian DTOs that was observed and reported by law enforcement agencies in 2008 continued to increase in 2009. Asian DTOs trafficked wholesale quantities of drugs in 24 of the 32 HIDTAs (see Map A2 in Appendix A), compared with 22 HIDTAs in 2007. Asian DTOs that had previously trafficked high-purity Southeast Asian heroin have become the predominant distributors of MDMA and high-potency marijuana, drugs typically associated with low criminal penalties and high profit margins. Asian DTOs increasingly smuggle large quantities of MDMA through and between ports of entry (POEs) along the U.S.–Canada border, as evidenced by seizure data that show a substantial increase in the amount of MDMA seized along the Northern Border from 2004 (312,389 dosage units) to 2009[8] (2,167,238 dosage units). While Asian DTOs continue to produce high-potency marijuana in Canada, they have decreased their reliance on foreign production by establishing marijuana grows in the United States, further reducing associated smuggling risks and costs. Consequently, the amount of marijuana seized along the U.S.–Canada border decreased from 10,447 kilograms in 2005 to 3,423 kilograms in 2009.

Asian DTOs have filled a niche by trafficking high-potency marijuana and MDMA—drugs not typically trafficked by Mexican, Colombian, or Dominican DTOs. This factor has contribute to their success; however, their success is largely due to their ability to estimate the risk and cost of engaging in any given criminal activity. Asian DTOs are willing to cooperate with other criminal groups to increase their profit and work with Caucasian, Hispanic, and African American DTOs or criminal groups in most major cities in an effort to expand their drug distribution and customer base.

Cuban DTOs and criminal groups are slowly expanding their drug trafficking activities beyond the Florida/Caribbean Region, in part by partnering with Mexican DTOs.

The influence of Cuban DTOs and criminal groups is expanding, albeit at a slower rate than that of Asian DTOs. The number of HIDTAs reporting Cuban DTO or criminal group activity increased from three in 2007 to eight in 2009. The expanding influence of Cuban DTOs and criminal groups is largely the result of their ability to exploit Cuban émigrés to establish and tend indoor marijuana grow sites in locations throughout the Florida/Caribbean and Southeast Regions (specifically in Alabama, Georgia, and North Carolina). Cuban DTO and criminal group activity also appears to be expanding in the Southwest Region, where law enforcement agencies in Arizona, New Mexico, and Texas report Cuban DTO or criminal group involvement in cocaine, heroin, methamphetamine, and marijuana trafficking. This expanding influence of Cuban DTOs and criminal groups can also be attributed to their close working relationships with Mexican DTOs. Many Cuban émigrés are brought illegally into the United States by smugglers who are associated with a Mexican DTO. Moreover, communities composed of both Cubans and Mexicans allow for the development of personal relationships between criminal groups. The full extent of these relationships is unknown. However, if they follow patterns similar to the relationships established between Mexican and Dominican DTOs, the involvement of Cuban DTOs and criminal groups in drug trafficking should expand further in the near term, although the threat posed by these groups will remain much lower than that posed by Mexican, Colombian, Dominican, and Asian DTOs.

DRUG TRAFFICKING BY CRIMINAL GANGS

There are nearly 1 million[9] active gang members in the United States, based on analysis of federal, state, and local data, and the involvement of criminal gangs in domestic drug trafficking is becoming increasingly complex. Since 2001, many gangs have advanced beyond their traditional role as local retail drug distributors in large cities to become more organized, adaptable, deliberate, and influential in large-scale drug trafficking (see Table B4 in Appendix B). Much of their growing influence has come at the expense of local independent dealers and small local criminal groups who cannot compete with gangs that establish control in smaller drug markets.

The influence of Hispanic and African American street gangs is expanding as these gangs gain greater control over drug distribution in rural and suburban areas and acquire drugs directly from DTOs in Mexico or along the Southwest Border.

In 2009, midlevel and retail drug distribution in the United States was dominated by more than 900,000 criminally active gang members representing approximately 20,000 domestic street gangs in more than 2,500 cities (see Map A3 in Appendix A). These street gangs vary greatly with respect to their ethnic or racial identities, the types and amounts of drugs that they distribute, their strength and influence, and their adaptability. Their prevalence varies geographically, with the greatest concentration of street gangs occurring in the Great Lakes, Pacific, Southeast, and Southwest OCDETF Regions (see Map A4 in Appendix A).

Many Hispanic and, to a lesser extent, African American gangs are gaining control over drug distribution outside urban areas that were previously supplied by local independent dealers or small local criminal groups. Around 2007, Hispanic and African American gangs throughout the country, but especially in the Southwest and Great Lakes Regions, began to command greater influence over drug distribution in many rural and suburban areas. This trend continued in 2009. For example, in 2009, the Avenues street gang based in Los Angeles, California, expanded its operations to distribute drugs in suburban and rural locations throughout southern California.

To increase their control over drug trafficking in smaller markets, street gangs have been increasingly acquiring larger wholesale quantities of drugs at lower prices directly from DTOs in Mexico and along the Southwest Border. Several Southwest Border street gangs, such as Shelltown 38th Street, Tri-City Bombers, and Vallucos, smuggle wholesale quantities of drugs obtained in Mexico into the United States. By purchasing directly from Mexican wholesale sources in Mexico or along the Southwest Border, gangs throughout the country realize cost savings that enable them to sell drugs at lower prices than local independent dealers in small communities, driving these dealers out of business. For example, members of the Chicago-based Latin Kings street gang who operate in Midland, Texas, purchase cocaine from Mexican traffickers in south Texas for $16,000 to $18,000 per kilogram, compared with $25,000 to $35,000 per kilogram from wholesale traffickers in Chicago. With this savings, the gang undersells other local dealers who do not have the capacity to buy large wholesale quantities directly from Mexican DTOs in Mexico or along the Southwest Border.

Hispanic prison gangs, primarily in Southwest Border states, are gaining strength by working directly with Mexican DTOs to acquire wholesale quantities of drugs and by controlling most street gangs in areas along the Southwest Border.

Prison gangs are active in all 50 states and are increasing their influence over drug trafficking in areas along the Southwest Border (see Table B4 in Appendix B). Prior to 2001, the criminal influence of prison gangs was limited primarily to retail-level drug distribution. However, since that time, Hispanic prison gangs have become increasingly involved in the transportation and wholesale distribution of drugs.

Hispanic prison gangs such as Hermanos de Pistoleros Latinos (HPL) and Raza Unida operating in Southwest Border states have increased their involvement in wholesale drug distribution activities through cooperative relationships with Mexican DTOs. Through these relationships, Hispanic prison gangs are able to gain access to wholesale quantities of drugs. For example, in September 2009, 21 members of HPL were convicted in the Southern District of Texas (Houston) of conspiring to distribute more than 150 kilograms of cocaine and laundering millions of dollars in drug proceeds. In April 2009, 15 members and associates of the Raza Unida prison gang were indicted for trafficking multikilogram quantities of cocaine and methamphetamine weekly in McAllen and Houston, Texas.

To ensure a consistent profit stream from the wholesale drugs that they purchase from Mexican DTOs, Hispanic prison gangs distribute drugs through street gangs that they largely, if not entirely, control. Through force or intimidation, Hispanic prison gangs exercise significant control over local gangs that distribute their drugs in the Southwest Border region. For example, Barrio Azteca prison gang members operating in El Paso, Texas, collect drug payments and taxes from 47 street-level gangs and independent drug dealers trafficking drugs in El Paso.

U.S. SOUTHWEST BORDER SMUGGLING AND VIOLENCE

Most illicit drugs available in the United States and thousands of illegal immigrants are smuggled into the United States across the nearly 2,000-mile Southwest Border, including through the Tohono O'odham Reservation (see text box on page 18). Conversely, a significant amount of illegal firearms and weapons as well as bulk currency are smuggled from the Southwest Border region into Mexico. Intensified counterdrug operations, in addition to intracartel and intercartel warfare and plaza competition, have resulted in unprecedented violence in northern Mexico and the potential for increasing violence in the United States.

Counterdrug operations on both sides of the Southwest Border have intensified in recent years, resulting in increased pressure on Mexican DTOs.

Several recent, large counterdrug initiatives in the United States and Mexico have been implemented to directly disrupt Mexican cartel operations. For example, in March 2008, the GOM initiated Operation Chihuahua in response to increased drug-related violence between the Juárez and Sinaloa Cartels over drug smuggling plazas in the Mexican border state of Chihuahua. Since then, more than 7,500 soldiers and 2,000 federal agents have been deployed to cities within the state, including Asunción, Buenaventura, Casas Grandes, Chihuahua City, Ciudad Juárez, Janos, Ojinaga, Nuevo Casas Grandes, and Palomas. Operation Chihuahua most likely resulted in seizures of drug shipments before they reached the U.S.–Mexico border, although official seizure statistics are not available. Similarly, the DEA-led Operation Xcellerator, which targeted the U.S. operations of the Sinaloa Cartel, concluded in November 2009 and resulted in 781 arrests and the seizure of more than 12,000 kilograms of cocaine, 17,000 pounds of marijuana, 1,200 pounds of methamphetamine, 1.3 million MDMA tablets, $61 million in U.S. currency, four aircraft, and three maritime vessels.

Mexican DTOs rely on overland transportation methods to smuggle drugs into the United States but also use alternative methods.

In addition to customary land smuggling practices, Mexican DTOs use alternative means to move contraband north across the border. These means include the construction and use of cross-border tunnels and subterranean passageways (see text box on page 15), and some increased use of low-flying small or ultralight aircraft, which most often are used to smuggle marijuana. For example, in the Yuma, Arizona, area, at least eight ultralight aircraft have been spotted since October 2008, after only sporadic reporting of such incidents along the entire border area in previous years. Additionally, in mid-November 2009, at least three suspected ultralight incursions were reported in New Mexico—two in Luna County and one in Hidalgo County.

Of some concern to law enforcement officials is the potential for cross-border drug smuggling routes to be used to move terrorists or weapons of mass destruction into the United States. However, there have been no documented incidents of this type involving Mexican DTOs, and according to federal law enforcement officials, the involvement of Mexican DTOs in this type of activity is very unlikely. Intelligence and law enforcement reporting indicates that DTOs have not demonstrated any interest in or intent to smuggle on behalf of terrorists.

TRAFFICKERS' USE OF SUBTERRANEAN TUNNELS ALONG THE SOUTHWEST BORDER

The number of tunnels extending from Mexico into the United States has increased, suggesting that DTOs consider these tunnels as useful investments to smuggle drugs into the United States. In fiscal year (FY) 2008, U.S. Customs and Border Protection (CBP) officers along the U.S.–Mexico border discovered 16 subterranean tunnels, the majority of which were in the Tucson Sector, which encompasses a border area of 262 miles from the New Mexico state line to Yuma County, Arizona. In FY2009, authorities discovered 26 subterranean tunnels, 20 of which were in the Tucson Sector, primarily in the area of Nogales. During this same period, CBP officers discovered 5 tunnels in California, 4 of which were located in the San Diego Sector. In February 2009, CBP initiated a program designed to impede the construction of tunnels in Nogales's extensive drainage system. The initiative involved the construction of a 12-foot-deep steel and concrete underground wall that extends 100 yards along the border near the DeConcini POE in Nogales.

Source: U.S. Customs and Border Protection; National Southwest Border Counternarcotics Strategy 2009.

Mexican DTOs use Southwest Border gangs to enforce and secure smuggling operations in Mexico and, to a lesser extent, the United States, particularly in California and Texas border areas.

Mexican DTOs employ gang members who collect unpaid debts by using threats, extortion, and intimidation and who murder rival traffickers or noncompliant members in Mexico and, to a far lesser extent, the United States. Mexican DTOs also use gang members to enforce control of drug trafficking routes from Mexico into the United States. Mexican DTOs have reportedly increased their efforts to recruit gang members along the Southwest Border. Gang members who are U.S. citizens are a particularly valuable asset to Mexican DTOs because they can normally cross the U. S.–Mexico border with less law enforcement scrutiny and therefore are less likely to have illicit drug loads interdicted.

Competition among rival Mexican drug cartels for control of several prominent smuggling plazas has caused a significant rise in the level of violence in Mexico and a potential rise in the United States.

In 2009, between 6,500 and 8,000 individuals (according to unofficial estimates) were murdered in Mexico as cartels battled for control over smuggling corridors and responded to increased pressure from the GOM. This high number of cartel-related murders reflects a steep increase over previous years. The most violent conflict is concentrated in, but not limited to, the Juárez Plaza. The Joaquín Guzmán-Loera Organization is challenging the Juárez Cartel for control of drug trafficking in the Juárez Plaza. Actions on the part of the Joaquín Guzmán-Loera organization and efforts by the Juárez Cartel to exercise greater control over the Juárez Plaza have resulted in increased violence between the two cartels.

Although much of the violence attributed to conflicts over control of smuggling routes has been confined to Mexico, some has occurred in the United States. Violence in the United States (see text box on page 16) has been limited primarily to attacks against alien smuggling organization (ASO) members and their families—some of whom have sought refuge from the violence in Mexico by moving to U.S. border communities such as Phoenix. For example, in recent years, kidnappings in Phoenix have numbered in the hundreds, with 260 in 2007, 299 in 2008, and 267 in 2009.

Often, the U.S. kidnapping victims have some connection to alien smuggling or local drug trafficking activities, although some are innocent family members or relatives of alien smugglers or drug traffickers. Kidnappings related to alien smuggling often occur because smugglers demand more money for their services. Kidnappings related to drug trafficking usually occur only as a direct result of localized drug trafficking activities. For example, an individual or individuals may be kidnapped because of a lost drug load or failure to pay a drug debt. The number of U.S. kidnapping incidents is most likely underreported because many victims' families are unwilling to report the crime for fear that the victim will be killed, the kidnappers will retaliate against the family, or law enforcement will discover the family's drug trafficking activities or illegal alien status.

VIOLENCE IN THE UNITED STATES

Direct violence similar to the conflicts occurring among major DTOs in Mexico is rare in the United States. Incidents of direct inter- cartel or intracartel violence have not materialized in the United States in a manner that in any way resembles the widespread cartel violence in Mexico. Nevertheless, some reports of DTO or cartel violence occasionally emerge, including some incidents in 2009. More typical, however, is indirect violence within DTOs or cartels. Indirect violence takes many forms: drug customers who owe money are kidnapped until payment is made and cartel employees who fail to deliver the contraband or the expected proceeds are disciplined through beatings, kidnappings, torture, or death.

Adding to the violence are assaults against U.S. law enforcement officers assigned to posts along the Southwest Border. While most of these assaults are related to alien smuggling activities, it is likely that some of the incidents are perpetrated by individuals involved in drug smuggling. Assaults against U.S. Border Patrol (USBP) agents increased 46 percent from 752 incidents in FY2006 to 1,097 incidents in FY2008. Contributing most to this increase were rocking[10] assaults, which rose 77 percent from 435 incidents in FY2006 to 769 incidents in FY2008. However, some assaults against USBP agents in California have been deadly, including the January 2008 murder of a USBP officer who was struck and killed by the automobile of a fleeing drug suspect in Imperial County and the fatal shooting of a USBP officer investigating suspicious activity in Campo in July 2009.

Weapons smuggled from the Southwest Border region to Mexico have contributed to the escalating violence in Mexico.

Thousands of weapons are smuggled from the United States to Mexico every year, according to the ATF. It is unclear how many of these weapons are smuggled into Mexico by DTOs or how many ultimately come into the possession of DTOs. Nevertheless, some percentage of this weapons smuggling is orchestrated by DTOs. The U.S. weapons that these DTOs acquire originate in cities in Arizona, California, and Texas. Mexican DTO-linked enforcement groups and gang members purchase firearms and ammunition from Federally Licensed Firearms Dealers at gun stores, gun shows, and pawn shops and from unlicensed dealers at gun shows, often using straw purchasers[11] to insulate themselves from the transactions. The firearms and ammunition are then smuggled from the United States to Mexico on behalf of Mexican DTOs.

The Southwest Border is a principal entry point into the United States for illegal aliens.

The Southwest Border region is the principal entry point for undocumented aliens smuggled from Mexico, Central America, and South America by ASOs. These ASOs often pay fees to Mexican DTOs for the right to operate along specific routes in certain border areas.

Additionally, some aliens who attempt to cross the U.S.–Mexico border illicitly each year and are encountered by law enforcement are from special-interest countries including Afghanistan, Iran, Iraq, and Pakistan. These special-interest aliens, numbering in the hundreds, constitute a very small fraction of annual apprehensions at the U.S.–Mexico border by law enforcement. Available reporting indicates that some alien smuggling organizations (ASOs) in Mexico specialize in moving special-interest aliens into the United States. However, among the aliens from special-interest countries who have been encountered at the U.S.–Mexico border over at least the past five years, none documented as a known or suspected terrorist has been identified as having been assisted by a DTO.

Of particular concern is the cross-border transit of criminal gang members who pose public safety threats to communities throughout the U.S.–Mexico border region and the country. These individuals include members of transnational gangs such as Barrio Azteca, Mara Salvatrucha (MS 13), and Sureños (including 18th Street, Florencia, and Los Wonders), who transit the

U.S.–Mexico border illicitly and smuggle drugs or weapons on behalf of Mexican DTOs.

THE ILLICIT DRUG THREAT IN INDIAN COUNTRY

The illicit drug threat in Indian Country varies by region and is influenced by the illicit drugs available in major cities near the reservations. Most illicit drugs available throughout Indian Country are transported to reservations by Native American criminal groups and independent dealers who travel to nearby cities to purchase drugs, primarily from Mexican DTOs and criminal groups. Traffickers also smuggle large amounts of illicit drugs, primarily marijuana, into the United States from Canada and Mexico through reservations that border these countries, namely the St. Regis Mohawk Reservation in New York, commonly referred to as the Akwesasne, and the Tohono O'odham Reservation in Arizona.

Multiple tons of high-potency marijuana are smuggled through the St. Regis Mohawk Reservation each week by Native American DTOs that are supplied by Canada-based DTOs. Native American DTOs also smuggle multithousand-tablet quantities of MDMA into the United States and multikilogram quantities of cocaine into Canada through the reservation. As much as 20 percent[a] of all high-potency marijuana produced in Canada each year is smuggled through the St. Regis Mohawk Reservation, which accounts for less than half a percent of the U.S.–Canada border. The shared international border and geography of the reservation make it conducive to cross-border drug trafficking activity while also inhibiting law enforcement interdiction efforts.

An estimated 5 to 10 percent[b] of all the marijuana produced in Mexico is transported by highly organized and compartmentalized Mexican DTOs each year through the Tohono O'odham Reservation, which accounts for less than 4 percent of the U.S.–Mexico border. These traffickers also smuggle lesser amounts of cocaine, heroin, and methamphetamine. Drug traffickers exploit the vast stretches of remote, sparsely populated desert, the 75 miles of largely unprotected border with Mexico, and the highways that connect the reservation to major metropolitan areas to distribute illicit drugs in markets throughout the United States.

a. NDIC-derived estimate based on law enforcement reporting and Royal Canadian Mounted Police production estimates.

b. NDIC-derived estimate based on law enforcement reporting and production estimates for Mexico.

DRUG MOVEMENT INTO AND WITHIN THE UNITED STATES

From January through November 2009, U.S. seizures of illegal drugs in transit exceeded 1,626 metric tons, indicating that DTOs succeed in moving several thousand tons of cocaine, methamphetamine, marijuana, heroin, and

MDMA into the United States annually. There are unique smuggling and transportation methods associated with each drug type, but overall, drug seizure data and law enforcement reporting indicate that overland smuggling and subsequent transportation by vehicle exceed all other methods combined (see Figure 1).

Overland Smuggling into the United States

Most foreign-produced illicit drugs available in the United States are smuggled into the country overland across the borders with Mexico and, to a much lesser extent, Canada (see Table 1 on page 20). Overland smuggling methods are relatively consistent (see text box on page 21); however, DTOs often shift routes in response to law enforcement pressure, intercartel conflicts or other external factors. Such shifts were observed in 2008 and 2009.

Some smuggling routes and methods for transporting cocaine, heroin, methamphetamine, and marijuana into the United States appear to have shifted, in part because of heightened law enforcement pressure, changes in drug production trends, and evolving market dynamics.

There have been significant and prolonged shifts in cocaine smuggling routes that most likely have been caused by a combination of factors, particularly decreased cocaine production in Colombia, but also enhanced counterdrug efforts in Mexico, high levels of cartel violence, sustained interdiction pressure, and cocaine flow to non-U.S. markets, especially Europe. In 2007, a decline in the amount of cocaine seized along the South-west Border in the South Texas region—the predominant cocaine smuggling route at the time—resulted in a sharp decline in the amount of cocaine seized overall. As seizure totals for South Texas declined, seizure totals for California POEs began trending upward. Since 2007, cocaine seizures at California POEs have equaled or exceeded seizure totals at South Texas POEs; nonetheless, overall seizure totals remain lower than the seizure totals recorded before the significant decline was noted. Although no single cause for the decline in overall seizures can be identified, multiple factors—including a sharp decline in cocaine production in 2008 (see Figure 7 on page 30) and enhanced GOM counterdrug efforts—likely contributed to the decrease in amounts being transported from South America to Mexico and ultimately to the Southwest Border. Moreover, several exceptionally large seizures of cocaine destined for

Mexico from South America in 2007 may have initiated the trend. These seizures coincide with the decline in seizures along the Southwest Border and were followed by an unprecedented decline in cocaine availability in many markets in the United States.

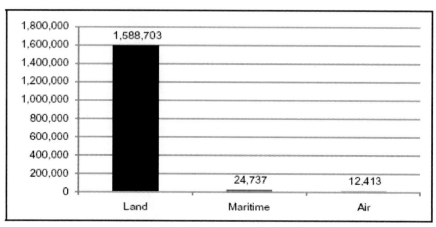

Source: National Seizure System.
*Data as of December 1, 2009; table includes seizures of cocaine, methamphetamine, marijuana, heroin, and MDMA.

Figure 1. Seizures of Drugs in Transit, Within the United States in Kilograms, 2009*.

Table 1. Drug Seizures Along the Southwest and Northern Borders in Kilograms, 2005–2009*.

	2005	**2006**	**2007**	**2008**	**2009**
Cocaine					
Southwest Border	22,653	28,284	22,656	16,755	17,085
Northern Border	>1	2	>1	>1	18
Total	22,654	28,286	22,657	16,756	17,103
Heroin					
Southwest Border	228	489	404	556	642
Northern Border	3	2	<1	<1	28
Total	231	491	405	557	670

Table 1. (Continued)

	2005	**2006**	**2007**	**2008**	**2009**
Marijuana					
Southwest Border	1,034,102	1,146,687	1,472,536	1,253,054	1,489,673
Northern Border	10,447	4,177	2,791	3,184	3,423
Total	1,044,549	1,150,864	1,475,327	1,256,238	1,493,096
MDMA					
Southwest Border	23	16	39	92	54
Northern Border	479	351	240	616	303
Total	502	367	279	708	357
Methamphetamine					
Southwest Border	2,918	2,798	1,860	2,201	3,478
Northern Border	>1	>1	136	>1	10
Total	2,919	2,799	1,996	2,202	3,488

Source: National Seizure System.
*Data as of December 1, 2009; totals are rounded to the nearest kilogram.

Conversely, heroin seizures along the South west Border have been increasing, most likely as a result of the growing Mexican influence in heroin production and transportation. This increase in Southwest Border heroin seizures coincides with a decrease in heroin seizures from commercial airlines. In 2008, the total amount of heroin seized along the Southwest Border (556.1 kg) exceeded the total amount of heroin seized from commercial airlines (398.1 kg) for the first time (see Table 2). This shift appears to be directly related to production trends and the changing roles of DTOs. For the past several years, production estimates for Mexican heroin, which is transported primarily overland across the Southwest Border, steadily increased to record levels in 2008. Furthermore, Mexican DTOs have become increasingly involved in the transportation of South American heroin. Meanwhile, production estimates for South American heroin, historically transported into the United States via commercial air, have steadily declined (see Figure 2 on page 24). This increased availability of Mexican heroin, coupled with increased involvement of Mexican DTOs in trafficking South American heroin, likely have resulted in significantly greater quantities of heroin being transported across the Southwest Border.

Methamphetamine and marijuana seizures have also increased along the Southwest Border, partly because of increased production. As with heroin, the increase appears to be specific to the drug. Methamphetamine production in Mexico appears to be increasing again after a sustained period of limited production resulting from laws that eventually banned pseudoephedrine in Mexico. Multiple factors may be contributing to an increase in marijuana smuggling, particularly decreased GOM cannabis eradication efforts, which have resulted in elevated production levels.

COMMON OVERLAND SMUGGLING METHODS

Mexican DTOs dominate the transportation of illicit drugs across the Southwest Border. They typically use commercial trucks and private and rental vehicles to smuggle cocaine, marijuana, methamphetamine, and heroin through the 25 land POEs as well as through vast areas of desert and mountainous terrain between POEs. Asian traffickers, OMGs, and Indo-Canadian drug traffickers transport significant quantities of high-potency marijuana and MDMA into the United States across the U.S.–Canada border. They use commercial trucks and private and rental vehicles to transport these drugs through more than 100 land POEs. They also use all-terrain vehicles (ATVs), aircraft, maritime vessels, and couriers on foot to smuggle drugs through vast areas between POEs.

A review of the smuggling patterns for each of the major drug types reveals myriad factors—some of which are interrelated and some of which are unique to the drug—that affect modes and methods used to transport drugs into the United States. Nonetheless, it is possible that seizures of large quantities of cocaine en route to Mexico and counterdrug efforts may have impacted the ability of major DTOs to smuggle cocaine from South America to Mexico. These factors may also explain the decrease in seizures along the Southwest Border, the decline in cocaine availability in portions of the United States, and the lack of similar long-term declines in the availability of methamphetamine, heroin, and marijuana.

Maritime Smuggling Directly into the United States

Significantly lesser quantities of drugs are smuggled directly into the United States by traffickers using maritime conveyances than by traffickers using overland routes. In 2009, less than 3 percent of all arrival zone drug seizures occurred on commercial and noncommercial maritime conveyances. Nevertheless, some DTOs continue to use maritime smuggling methods to move illegal drugs into the United States (see text box on page 22), and like overland smugglers, some of these maritime smugglers shifted their operations in 2008 and 2009 in response to law enforcement pressure or gaps in interdiction coverage.

Traffickers used private maritime vessels to smuggle drugs into the United States during 2009 through Puerto Rico, South Florida, South Texas, and southern California, and Mexican DTOs sometimes smuggle drugs by maritime means to avoid law enforcement scrutiny along the Southwest Border.

The primary threat from drug smuggling via private vessels is from Caribbean-based traffickers exploiting the Puerto Rico and Florida coastlines. Traffickers transported mostly cocaine from the Dominican Republic to Puerto Rico, although they smuggled lesser amounts of heroin and MDMA, sometimes commingled with cocaine loads. Caribbean traffickers also smuggled cocaine, heroin, and marijuana from the Bahamas to areas of South Florida between Miami and Palm Beach. Seizure totals and routes remained relatively constant compared with those of previous years.

COMMON MARITIME SMUGGLING METHODS

Various DTOs—most notably Colombian but also Dominican, Jamaican, Puerto Rican, and Venezuelan—transport cocaine and lesser amounts of heroin and marijuana to the United States using a variety of conveyances, including container ships, cruise ships, commercial fishing vessels, recreation vessels, and go-fast boats. The drugs are typically concealed in hidden compartments, commingled with legitimate goods, or couriered by passenger or crew members on maritime vessels. Traffickers also have increasingly used self-propelled semisubmersibles (SPSSs)[a] to transport cocaine from South America to Mexico. The use of SPSSs affords traffickers the ability to covertly transport large quantities of drugs.

a. Self-propelled semisubmersible vessels are maritime vessels used by traffickers to transport illicit drugs. These vessels typically protrude only a few inches above the surface of the water, making them very difficult to detect visually. SPSSs typically have a four-man crew and are capable of carrying multiton quantities of cocaine.

Mexican traffickers seeking to avoid scrutiny along the Southwest Border used private vessels to smuggle marijuana and cocaine into the United States during 2009. Incidents involving kilogram packages of cocaine and marijuana washing up or being found abandoned along the South Texas coastline increased, particularly in the South Padre Island area, during the first half of the year. By the end of December, more than 114 kilograms of cocaine had been recovered in the region. In comparison, only 1 kilogram was recovered in the region during 2008. Federal investigators believe that the smugglers typically depart from Tamaulipas State in northern Mexico and make short hops to the Texas coastline. Mexican traffickers also used private vessels in 2009 to smuggle marijuana from the northern Mexico state of Baja California to southern California. In fact, in 2009, more than 3.1 metric tons of marijuana were reported to have been seized from private vessels arriving in southern California, primarily the San Diego area.

Commercial maritime vessels, especially maritime containers, remain a viable conveyance for smuggling drugs directly into the United States, but seizure data and law enforcement reporting indicate that this smuggling method continues to account for a relatively small portion of the nation's illicit drug supply.

Traffickers use commercial maritime vessels to smuggle sizable quantities of drugs into the United States, but data suggest that other conveyance methods are preferred by smugglers. Traffickers often hide drugs among legitimate cargo in maritime containers, a fraction of which are inspected. Analysis of commercial maritime seizure data for 2004 through 2009 indicates that cocaine and marijuana are most often smuggled in commercial maritime vessels from Caribbean locations, such as the Dominican Republic, Haiti, and Jamaica, into East Coast ports in Florida and New Jersey. Traffickers also use commercial vessels to smuggle cocaine from the Dominican Republic into

Puerto Rico. Smaller amounts of heroin, typically 2 kilograms or less, are occasionally smuggled by cruise ship passengers working for Caribbean trafficking organizations into East Coast ports; however, this smuggling technique appears to have declined since 2006. Seizure data indicate that methamphetamine is rarely smuggled into the United States on commercial maritime vessels.

THE LOGISTICS OF TRANSPORTING DRUG SHIPMENTS

DTOs have well-established transportation networks and often transport illicit drug shipments directly to drug markets throughout the United States. Some DTOs relinquish control by distributing illicit drugs from stash locations to traffickers who purchase these drugs and then transport the shipments themselves to distribution areas. DTOs often hire independent drug transportation groups to transport drugs, insulating themselves from law enforcement investigations and compartmentalizing trafficking operations. These transporters are hired for the sole purpose of moving drug shipments, and they operate in cells that are separate from other DTO operations. As a result, seizures of illicit drugs from transporters often yield little or no information to law enforcement officials about other DTO members or DTO operations. For example, Colombian DTOs often employ Mexican traffickers whose successful transportation networks allow these DTOs to circumvent the problems caused by law enforcement disruption of their own transportation routes.

Drug shipments are typically stashed in ranches, warehouses, residences, and trailers near primary points of entry into the United States for consolidation, distribution, and subsequent transport to drug markets throughout the United States. To transport drugs, traffickers primarily use commercial trucks and privately owned and rental vehicles equipped with hidden compartments and natural voids in the vehicles. Additionally, bulk quantities of illicit drugs are sometimes commingled with legitimate goods in commercial trucks. Many drug traffickers use postal and package delivery services to transport illicit drugs within the United States and, to a much lesser extent, use couriers and cargo shipments on aircraft, buses, and trains.

Despite the fact that sizable quantities of drugs are seized annually from commercial maritime vessels arriving in the United States, the dominance of

Mexican trafficking organizations as the primary transporters of cocaine, heroin, marijuana, and meth-amphetamine to the United States results in commercial maritime seizure totals that are far less than Southwest Border seizure totals. Seizure data for 2009 show that the amount seized from commercial maritime vessels remains less than 1 percent (6,015 kg of 828,223 kg) of the amount seized at the Southwest Border. Law enforcement reporting confirms that Caribbean and South American traffickers are more likely than Mexican traffickers to take advantage of commercial maritime vessels as a smuggling conveyance to supply their much smaller U.S. distribution networks. Moreover, large quantities of drugs seized at U.S. ports are often destined for distribution in countries other than the United States. Many drug shipments concealed in commercial maritime containers by Caribbean and South American traffickers are intercepted by U.S. authorities as they transit the United States en route to markets in Europe and Asia.

Table 2. Heroin Seizures at Southwest Border Area and Commercial Air POEs, in Kilograms, 2004–2009*

	2004	2005	2006	2007	2008	2009*
Southwest Border	386	229	489	362	556	642
Commercial Air POEs	909	740	529	424	398	199

Source: National Seizure System.
*Data as of December 1, 2009.

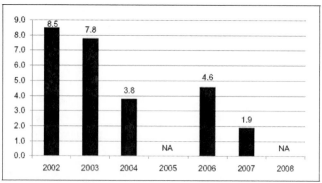

Source: U.S. Government estimate.
*Estimated figure for 2007 based on partial data because of incomplete survey; estimates for 2005 and 2008 not available.

Figure 2. Potential Pure Heroin Production Estimates, Colombia, in Metric Tons, 2002–2008*.

Table 3. Metropolitan Areas Most Often Identified as Origination and Destination Points for Seized Drug Shipments, by Drug, 2008–2009*.

	Cannabis	Cocaine	Heroin	Methamphetamine	MDMA
Origination	McAllen Phoenix Tucson Rio Grande City Laredo	McAllen Los Angeles Phoenix Houston Laredo	Denver Phoenix Miami Chicago Orlando	Phoenix Los Angeles McAllen San Bernardino Seattle	Los Angeles New York Seattle Lynden (WA) Detroit
Destination	Houston Chicago Atlanta Tucson Detroit	Atlanta Chicago New York Miami Houston	Chicago New York Miami Newark Tacoma	Atlanta Sacramento Las Vegas Denver Chicago	New York Houston Baton Rouge Ocala (FL) Atlanta

Source: National Seizure System.
*Data as of June 30, 2009.

Air Smuggling into the United States

The amount of drugs smuggled into the United States by couriers and in cargo aboard commercial aircraft is significantly less than the amount smuggled by other means. In 2009, the total amount seized from commercial aircraft for cocaine, heroin, methamphetamine, marijuana, and MDMA was less than for any other conveyance. Drug seizure data show that only 24 percent of heroin seizures, 15 percent of MDMA seizures, 6 percent of cocaine seizures and less than 1 percent each of meth-amphetamine and marijuana seizures were from commercial air conveyances.

The use of commercial air to smuggle heroin into the United States is rapidly declining, while heroin smuggling over the Southwest Border is increasing.

The amount of heroin seized at commercial air POEs decreased 56.2 percent (909 kg to 398 kg) from 2004 through 2008. The decrease is partially attributable to a shift in the smuggling of South American heroin by couriers on commercial flights to overland transportation across the Southwest Border as well as increased airport interdiction activities in Colombian airports. Colombian DTOs are now, to a large extent, relying on Mexican DTOs to smuggle heroin overland into the United States rather than conducting their own air courier smuggling operations. At the same time that heroin seizures decreased at commercial air POEs, heroin seizures at Southwest Border POEs increased 44.0 percent (386 kg to 556 kg), and preliminary seizure data indicate that Southwest Border heroin seizures reached a record high in 2009 (see Table 2 on page 24).

The decline in commercial air smuggling for heroin is attributable to a number of factors, including decreasing South American heroin production and a shift to smuggling routes across the Southwest Border. Most of the heroin seized at air POEs in previous years was seized from South American heroin couriers. However, South American heroin production appears to have decreased sharply since 2003 (see Figure 2 on page 24).

The Flow of Drugs Within the United States

There are 327 official U.S. land, maritime, and air POEs; however, a relatively few POEs account for most of the drug flow into the United States. In fact, 88 percent of all drug seizures occurred at just 20 POEs. From these and other POEs, drug shipments are transported to dozens of national and regional distribution centers through eight principal corridors to the major drug markets within the United States. (See Figure 3 on page 26.)

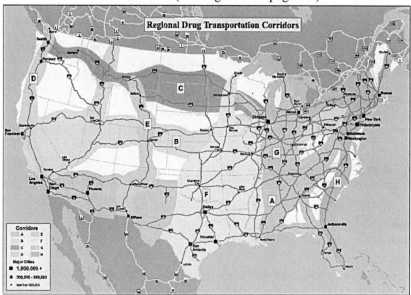

Source: Federal, state, and local law enforcement data and reporting.

Figure 3. Drug Transportation Corridors in the United States.

Among the eight principal drug corridors, Corridor A is particularly vital to DTOs. Corridor A is the primary route for DTOs transporting multiton quantities of cocaine, heroin, marijuana, and methamphetamine from the Southwest Border to eastern U.S. drug markets, many of the largest drug markets in the country. Within Corridor A, Interstate 10 as well as Interstates 8 and 20 are among those most used by drug couriers, as evidenced by drug seizure data showing that from 2008 through October 2009, nearly 19 percent of all reported interstate cocaine seizures and 7 percent of all reported interstate heroin seizures occurred on these routes.

Corridor B is also important to DTOs, especially those moving methamphetamine and marijuana produced in California or Mexico to major market areas in western, central, or eastern states. Interstates 15, 80, 70, and 40 are the leading routes through Corridor B, and seizures on these interstates accounted for 46 percent of all reported methamphetamine seizures and 31 percent of all marijuana seizures on interstates from 2008 through October 2009.

Drug couriers moving drugs through the various corridors are often destined for one of the relatively few primary U.S. drug markets, where there are large drug user populations and where drugs are further distributed to smaller markets. There are relatively little data available to objectively rank cities as leading or lesser drug markets. Nevertheless, analysis of national seizure data that identify the destination and origination of drug shipments shows that seven city areas (Chicago, Denver, Detroit, Houston, Miami, New York, and Tucson) are identified more often than any other cities as major points of both origination[12] and destination for drug shipments (see Table 3 on page 24).

DRUG AVAILABILITY IN THE UNITED STATES

There are no current estimates for the amount of drugs available in U.S. drug markets, nor are there sufficient data to more accurately measure quantities of specific drugs nationally. Thus, a determination of whether drug availability is increasing or decreasing is based on analysis of indicator data, including foreign and domestic production estimates, price and purity data, seizure data, transportation and distribution trends, and demand data.[13] These indicator data show that in 2009, cocaine availability was decreasing, while heroin, marijuana, methamphetamine, and MDMA remained readily available, with increases in some areas.

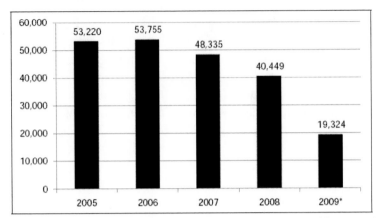

Source: National Drug Intelligence Center analysis of Federal-Wide Drug Seizure
  System data.
*Data as of June 2009.
Note: Federal-wide Drug Seizure System totals have been adjusted to exclude seizures
  that did not occur within the United States or its territorial waters.

Figure 4. Federal Cocaine Seizure Totals, in Kilograms, 2005–2009*.

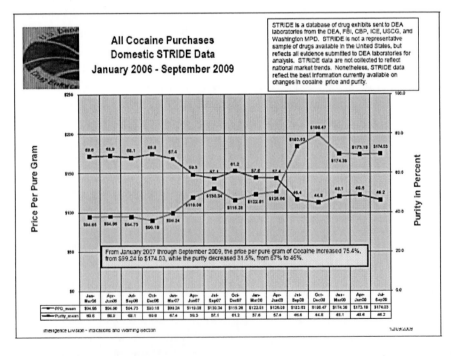

Figure 5. Cocaine Price and Purity Data.

Cocaine Availability

Cocaine availability has decreased sharply in the United States since 2006. Every national- level cocaine availability data indicator (seizures, price, purity, workplace drug tests, and ED data) points to significantly less availability in 2009 than in 2006. For example, federal cocaine seizures decreased 25 percent from 2006 (53,755 kg) to 2008 (40,449 kg) and remained low in 2009 (see Figure 4). The price per pure gram of cocaine increased from $94.73 in the third quarter of 2006 to $174.03 in the third quarter of 2009, while cocaine purity decreased from 68.1 percent to 46.2 percent (see Figure 5 on page 28).

Workplace drug tests also indicated a reduction in cocaine availability; the percentage of positive tests for cocaine among samples submitted to Quest Diagnostics declined substantially between the end of 2006 and midyear 2009 (see Figure 6 on page 28). In addition, all 14 cities monitored by DAWN reported that the proportion of drug-related emergency department admissions attributed to cocaine has declined since 2006.

Anecdotal reporting from law enforcement officials throughout the country supports the trend reflected in the national data. Of the 51 U.S. drug markets where cocaine availability is closely monitored, officials in 22 drug markets (primarily markets east of the Mississippi River and along the Southwest Border) report that during the first half of 2009, availability was below 2006 levels; the cocaine shortages have been attributed to several factors (see text box). Officials in only 4 of the 51 markets—Boise, Idaho; Omaha, Nebraska; Portland, Oregon; and Salt Lake City, Utah— reported that cocaine availability levels were higher than in 2006.

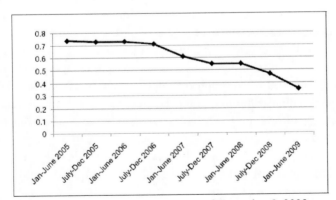

Source: Quest Diagnostics Incorporated. *Data as of December 9, 2009.

Figure 6. National Cocaine Positivity Rates in Workplace Drug Tests, 2005–2009*.

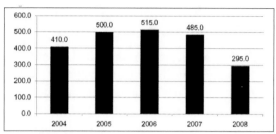

Source: U.S. Government estimate.

Figure 7. Potential Pure Cocaine Production in Colombia, in Metric Tons, 2004–2008.

POTENTIAL CAUSES FOR COCAINE SHORTAGES IN U.S. DRUG MARKETS

Although no single factor for the decline in cocaine availability can be identified, a combination of factors, including increased law enforcement efforts in Mexico and the transit zones, decreased cocaine production in Colombia, high levels of cartel violence, and cocaine flow to non-U.S. markets likely contributed to decreased amounts being transported to the U.S.–Mexico border for subsequent smuggling into the United States. Cocaine production estimates for Colombia decreased slightly in 2007 and significantly in 2008 (see Figure 7 on page 30), reducing the amount of cocaine available to world markets. Traffickers in Bolivia and Peru produced sizable quantities of cocaine during the 2-year period, but their estimated production capability and well-established trafficking networks would not be able to quickly fill voids in the U.S. cocaine supply caused by the decline in Colombian production. Moreover, during 2007, several exceptionally large seizures of cocaine destined for Mexico may have initiated the first reported cocaine shortages in U.S. drug markets. These seizures coincided with the decline in seizures along the Southwest Border and were followed by an unprecedented decline in cocaine availability, a trend that continued through 2009. Helping to sustain the shortages were counterdrug efforts on both sides of the border, which most likely diminished the ability of one or more major DTOs to obtain cocaine from South America for subsequent distribution in the United States. Finally, expanding world markets for cocaine in Europe (a highly profitable mar-ket) and South America may be further reducing the already reduced amount available from Colombian sources to distribute in the United States.

Heroin Availability

Heroin remains widely available in many U.S. drug markets; availability is increasing in some areas.

Law enforcement reporting indicates that heroin remains widely available and that availability is increasing in some areas, as evidenced by high wholesale purity, low prices, increased levels of abuse, and elevated numbers of heroin-related overdoses and overdose deaths. For instance, according to DEA Heroin Signature Program (HSP) data, the wholesale purity of Mexican heroin was 40 percent in 2008, the highest average purity for Mexican heroin analyzed under the HSP since 2005 (47%). Additionally, Mexican heroin represented 39 percent (by weight) of all heroin analyzed through the HSP, the highest percentage since 1987 (42%). The wholesale purity of South American heroin stabilized at 57 percent in 2008 after significantly decreasing from 2000 to 2006. However, South American heroin representation under the HSP decreased markedly to 58 percent (by weight) in 2008 from a high of 88 percent in 2003. The decreased representation of South American heroin under the HSP resulted from a significant increase of Mexican heroin samples seized and analyzed under the program, 300 kilograms in 2008 compared with 136 kilograms in 2007, rather than an overall decrease in South American heroin samples. In fact, South American heroin samples analyzed under the HSP increased from 424 kilograms in 2007 to 442 kilograms in 2008.

Increased availability in some markets can be partly attributed to increased heroin production in Mexico. From 2004 through 2008, heroin production estimates for Mexico increased 342 percent, from 8.6 metric tons pure to 38 metric tons pure (see Figure 8 on page 31).

Increased heroin availability has led to increased heroin abuse and, consequently, an increase in heroin-related overdoses and overdose deaths. Law enforcement reporting from the Great Lakes, Mid-Atlantic, New England, New York/New Jersey, Southeast, and West Central OCDETF Regions suggests that heroin abuse is increasing, particularly among younger abusers. Moreover, in mid-2009, law enforcement and public health agencies in 29 drug markets spanning 17 states began reporting elevated levels of heroin-related overdoses, which in many areas began to increase in 2008 (see Figure 9 on page 31). The degree to which heroin overdoses increased in these drug markets—which ranged in size from Burlington, Vermont, to Dallas, Texas— varied widely, but for each area the increase was significant relative to what local officials normally observe. Although a variety of factors have been associated with the increase, including some prescription opioid users switching to heroin (see text box), the only commonality appears to be an overall increase in heroin availability.

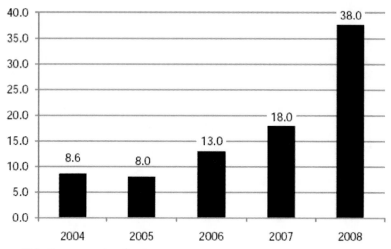

Source: U.S. Government estimate.

Figure 8. Potential Pure Heroin Production in Mexico in Metric Tons, 2004–2008.

Figure 9. Counties Reporting Increases in Heroin-Related Overdoses, 2008–2009.

PRESCRIPTION OPIOID USERS HAVE SWITCHED TO HEROIN

Some opioid abusers use prescription opioids or heroin, depending on availability and the price of each drug, and heroin availability is increasing in many regions in response to higher demand. Treatment providers in some areas of the United States reported in 2008 that prescription opioid abusers switch to heroin as they build tolerance to prescription opioids and seek a more euphoric high. Further, treatment providers are reporting that some prescription opioid abusers are switching to heroin in a few areas where heroin is less costly or more available than prescription opioids. It is also common for some heroin abusers to use prescription opioids when they cannot obtain heroin. Diverted CPDs are often more readily available than heroin in all drug markets; however, heroin use increased in many areas of the country in 2009, possibly because of increased demand among abusers of prescription opioids who could no longer afford CPDs. Prescription opioids are typically more expensive than heroin. For example, oxycodone abusers with a high tolerance may ingest 400 milligrams of the drug daily (five 80-mg tablets) for an average daily cost of $400. These abusers could maintain their addictions with 2 grams of heroin daily, at a cost of one-third to one- half that of prescription opioids, depending on the area of the country and the purity of the heroin.

The capacity of Mexican DTOs to occupy a more significant share of the heroin market in cities historically dominated by South American heroin may be evolving. In addition to Mexican DTOs trafficking and distributing greater quantities of South American heroin, investigative reporting and heroin signature analysis indicate the possibility of white heroin being produced in Mexico using Colombian processing techniques, as well as the distribution of "mixed" heroin containing both South American and Mexican heroin. However, additional information is needed to confirm the existence of and to understand the potential threat posed by these two heroin forms.

Despite record estimates of opium and heroin production in Afghanistan, the United States remains a secondary market for Southwest Asian (SWA) heroin. SWA heroin is smuggled into the United States in relatively small quantities, primarily by couriers on transatlantic flights and through the international mail system. Organizations responsible for trafficking SWA heroin into the United States are based primarily in Afghanistan, Pakistan,

West Africa, and India. Similarly, even though Southeast Asian (SEA) opium and heroin production estimates marginally increased from 2007 to 2008, only limited quantities of the drug are available in the United States. Most SEA heroin is consumed regionally in Southeast Asia and the East Asia–Pacific region.

Methamphetamine Availability

From mid-2008 through 2009, methamphetamine availability increased in the United States. Drug availability indicator data show that methamphetamine prices, which peaked in 2007, declined significantly during 2008 and 2009, while methamphetamine purity increased (see Figure 10 on page 33). Methamphetamine seizures also increased in 2008 after dropping in 2007, and 2009 data indicate that seizures continue to rise (see Figure 11 on page 33).

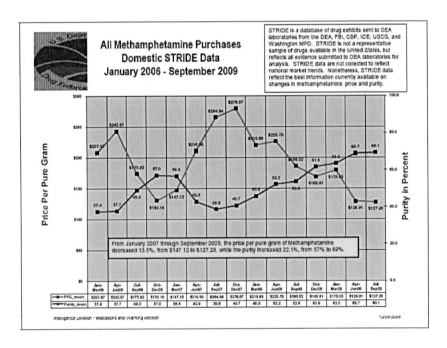

Figure 10. Methamphetamine Price and Purity Data.

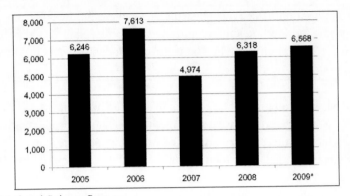

Source: National Seizure System.
*Data as of December 1, 2009.

Figure 11. Methamphetamine Seizure Amounts in the United States, in Kilograms 2005–2009*.

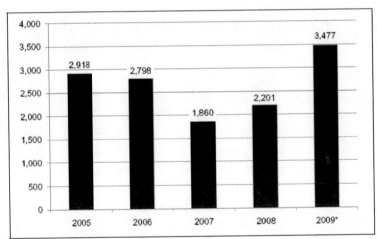

Source: National Seizure System. *Data as of December 1, 2009.

Figure 12. Southwest Border Methamphetamine Seizure Amounts, in Kilograms 2005–2009*.

METHAMPHETAMINE CHEMICAL RESTRICTIONS IN MEXICO

Pseudoephedrine and ephedrine import restrictions in Mexico resulted in decreased Mexican methamphetamine production in 2007 and 2008. In 2005, the GOM began implementing progressively increasing restrictions on the importation of pseudoephedrine and ephedrine. In 2007, the GOM announced a prohibition on pseudoephedrine and ephedrine imports into Mexico for 2008 meth and a ban on the use of both chemicals in Mexico by 2009.

Analysis of available data indicates that methamphetamine availability in the United States is directly related to methamphetamine production trends in Mexico, which is the primary source of methamphetamine consumed in the United States. That is, as methamphetamine production declined in Mexico in 2007 and early 2008 as a result of precursor chemical restrictions (see text box), methamphetamine availability declined in the United States. By late 2008, however, Mexican DTOs had adapted their operating procedures in several ways including the smuggling of restricted chemicals via new routes, importing nonrestricted chemical derivatives instead of precursor chemicals, and using alternative production methods. For example, Mexican DTOs smuggle ephedrine and pseudoephedrine from source areas in China and India using indirect smuggling routes that include transit through Central Africa, Europe, and South America. In addition, packages containing ephedrine and pseudoephedrine are commonly mislabeled as other items during transit to avoid law enforcement inspection at air and seaports in Mexico. Methamphetamine producers in Mexico also have begun importing chemical derivatives such as n-acetyl ephedrine and methylamine that are not regulated in Mexico, but can be used to produce methamphetamine precursor chemicals and ultimately methamphetamine. Limited access to ephedrine and pseudoephedrine has also prompted meth- amphetamine producers in Mexico to increasingly use nonephedrine-based methamphetamine production methods. According to DEA reporting, Mexican DTOs conduct large-scale nonephedrine-based production operations in Mexico, particularly using the phenyl-2-propanone (P2P) method. In fact, the GOM has reported several seizures of phenylacetic acid, a chemical used to produce the methamphetamine precursor chemical P2P. Circumventing the chemical control laws in Mexico has enabled an upsurge in methamphetamine production in Mexico and increased the flow of methamphetamine into the United States as evidenced by methamphetamine seizures at or between POEs along the U.S.– Mexico border (see Figure 12).

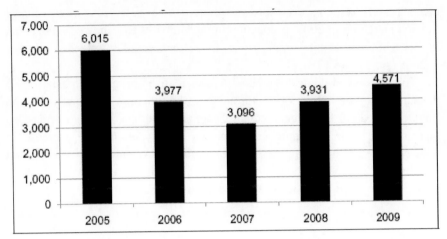

Source: National Seizure System.

Figure 13. Methamphetamine Laboratory Seizures, 2005–2009.

RESTRICTIONS ON THE RETAIL SALES OF PSEUDOEPHEDRINE

In September 2006, the federal Combat Methamphetamine Epidemic Act (CMEA) of 2005 became effective nationwide, setting restrictions on the retail sale of pseudoephedrine products. As of December 2009, 45 states had passed measures establishing or enhancing restrictions on over-the-counter sales or purchases of pseudoephedrine products in addition to those set forth by the CMEA. Of those states, 20 made pseudoephedrine a scheduled[a] drug, 43 have imposed point-of-sale restrictions, and 26 have enacted pseudoephedrine tracking laws (see Table B5 in Appendix B).

a. The legal implications of a given schedule may vary from state to state; states that classify the same substance in the same schedule do not necessarily regulate that substance the same way. Some states that schedule pseudoephedrine also exempt certain forms, such as those in liquid form or those a designated state authority has determined cannot be used to make methamphetamine. As a result, in some cases, states that do not schedule pseudoephedrine may still regulate it as strictly as or more so than states that do.

When methamphetamine production in Mexico was disrupted in 2007 and 2008, production in the United States increased as users and distributors compensated for the reduced foreign supply. However, even as production in Mexico increased in 2009, production in the United States showed no decline. In fact, U.S. methamphetamine laboratory seizures in 2009 exceeded seizures in 2008 (see Figure 13).

The increase in domestic production was realized primarily in small-scale methamphetamine laboratories throughout the country, especially in the Southeast Region; however, methamphetamine superlabs[14] in California also increased in scale and number during the same period. The increase in domestic meth- amphetamine production in 2008 and 2009 was fueled primarily by individuals and criminal groups that organized pseudoephedrine smurfing15 operations to acquire large amounts of the chemical.

Marijuana Availability

Marijuana is widely available, in part as a result of rising production in Mexico. The amount of marijuana produced in Mexico has increased an estimated 59 percent overall since 2003 (see Figure 14). Contributing to the increased production in Mexico is a decrease in cannabis eradication (see text box), which has resulted in significantly more marijuana being smuggled into the United States from Mexico, as evidenced by a sharp rise in border seizures (see Figure 15).

CANNABIS ERADICATION IN MEXICO IS DECREASING

Despite rising marijuana cultivation and production in Mexico, the amount of cannabis eradicated decreased by 48 percent from 2006 (30,162 hectares) to 2008 (15,756 hectares); eradication in 2009 is expected to be low as well. The reduction is the result of the Mexican military's focus on antiviolence measures rather than illicit crop cultivation.

Mexican DTOs have expanded their cultivation operations into the United States, an ongoing trend for the past decade. Nonetheless, cultivation operations in some areas of the country have been hindered by intensified eradication efforts. In addition, law enforcement pressure may be limiting the amount produced domestically by some DTOs, resulting in heightened smuggling from Mexico.

The amount of marijuana produced domestically is unknown.[16] However, eradication data and law enforcement reporting indicate that the amount of marijuana produced in the United States appears to be very high, based in part on the continual increases in the number of plants eradicated nationally (see Table 4). In fact, eradication of plants from both indoor and outdoor sites has more than doubled since 2004. Well-organized criminal groups and DTOs that produce domestic marijuana do so because of the high profitability of and demand for marijuana in the United States. These groups have realized the benefits of producing large quantities of marijuana in the United States, including having direct access to a large customer base, avoiding the risk of detection and seizure during transportation across the U.S.–Canada and U.S.–Mexico borders, and increasing profits by reducing transportation costs.

Marijuana is produced in the United States by various DTOs and criminal groups, including Caucasian, Asian, and Mexican groups, but Caucasian independents and criminal groups are well established in every region of the country and very likely produce the most marijuana domestically overall.[17] Mexican, Asian, and Cuban criminal groups and DTOs, in particular, pose an increasing threat in regard to domestic cultivation, since their cultivation activities often involve illegal immigrants and large-scale growing operations ranging from 100 to more than 1,000 plants per site. In addition, these groups appear to be expanding and shifting operations within the United States (see text box on page 49).

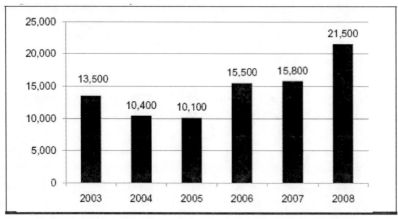

Source: U.S. Government estimate.

Figure 14. Potential Marijuana Production in Mexico, in Metric Tons, 2003–2008.

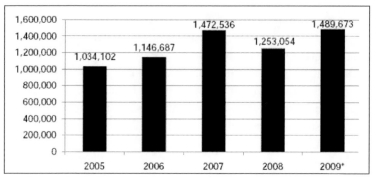

Source: National Seizure System. *Data as of December 1, 2009.

Figure 15. Southwest Border Area Marijuana Seizures, in Kilograms, 2005–2009*.

Significant quantities of cannabis are cultivated on public lands, particularly by Mexican DTOs and criminal groups, as evidenced by high and increasing eradication figures. Over the past 5 years, more than 11 million marijuana plants (see Table 5) have been eradicated from federal public lands—the majority were eradicated from public lands in western states. In addition, the number of plants eradicated from these lands increased more than 300 percent from 1,013,088 plants in 2004 to 4,043,231 plants in 2008. Public lands are often used for cannabis cultivation because DTOs benefit from the remote locations that seemingly limit the chance of detection and allow them to maintain such activities without ownership of any land that can be seized by law enforcement or traced back to a participating member. The increased prevalence of these grow sites on publicly accessible lands has resulted in numerous armed confrontations with hikers, hunters, and passersby unwittingly entering active cultivation sites.

More growers are establishing indoor grow sites to produce better marijuana and avoid outdoor detection and eradication.

Indoor cannabis cultivation that allows for increased security and potentially higher-quality marijuana has become more popular—particularly with Caucasian independents and criminal groups—with the proliferation of coordinated outdoor eradication efforts nationwide (see Table 4 and Table 5). Law enforcement attributes the increased interest in cultivating indoors partially to the heightened levels of outdoor eradication. However, some groups— particularly Asian groups—have established large-scale operations in, or shifted operations to, the United States to avoid seizure of the shipments

at the Canadian border and to attain better access to drug markets. In addition
to the increased sense of security that indoor sites provide, cultivators benefit
from year-round production and controlled environmental conditions such as
lighting and nutrients. Controlling these factors allows for increased growth
and maturation times, as well as potentially higher- quality marijuana that can
command a much higher price.

**Table 4. Number of Plants Eradicated From Indoor and Outdoor Sites
in the United States, 2004–2008.**

	2004	2005	2006	2007	2008
Indoor	203,896	270,935	400,892	434,728	450,986
Outdoor	2,996,225	3,938,151	4,830,766	6,599,599	7,562,322
Total	3,200,121	4,209,086	5,231,658	7,034,327	8,013,308

Source: Domestic Cannabis Eradication/Suppression Program (DCE/SP).

Note: DEA methodology for collecting DCE/SP data changed in 2007. Since 2007,
public lands data have been included in the number of outdoor plants eradicated
and therefore should not be compared with previous years' data.

Table 5. Number of Plants Eradicated From Federal Lands, 2004–2008*.

	2004	2005	2006	2007	2008
Forest Service	718,447	992,264	1,245,324	2,176,952	3,079,923*
U.S. Department of the Interior	294,641	263,005	590,352	715,071	963,308*

Source: U.S. Department of Agriculture Forest Service; U.S. Department of the
Interior.

*Forest Service data as of February 12, 2009; U.S. Department of the Interior data as of
January 21, 2009.

CRIMINAL GROUPS AND DTOS EXPANDING DOMESTIC CANNABIS CULTIVATION OPERATIONS AT BOTH INDOOR AND OUTDOOR SITES

Mexican traffickers are expanding and shifting outdoor cultivation
operations eastward across the United States into areas that they believe are
less subject to law enforcement scrutiny. These Mexican DTOs have
established cultivation operations in areas outside their traditional
strongholds of California, Washington, and Oregon. Since 1999, law

enforcement reporting has noted this eastward shift and expansion from these western states to Arizona, Arkansas, Georgia, Idaho, North Carolina, Tennessee and, most recently, Wisconsin and Michigan. These groups appear to be moving to these areas in response to improved outdoor grow site detection capabilities and heightened eradication efforts.

Asian traffickers are operating an increasing number of indoor grow sites. Some U.S.-based and Canada-based Asian groups (primarily ethnic Vietnamese and Chinese) engage in large-scale indoor cultivation, operating multithousand plant sites, predominantly in the Pacific Northwest and throughout much of California. Within the past decade, these tight-knit and often family-oriented groups have expanded their network throughout the country to numerous states, including Texas and several New England states, to avoid law enforcement detection and to gain better access to drug markets.

Cuban traffickers are the primary operators of indoor marijuana grow sites in the Southeast Region. Cuban-operated indoor sites are of a smaller scale than Asian-operated grows. Cannabis cultivation sites operated by Cuban traffickers are most prevalent in southern Florida, but such activity has expanded northward into northern Florida, Georgia, and North Carolina to move operations closer to potential drug markets. Cuban immigrants are often exploited by DTOs and criminal groups to cultivate high-potency cannabis at these indoor sites, and the problem appears to be growing. Law enforcement reporting and eradication data indicate an increase in the seizure of indoor cannabis grow operations that cultivate high-potency marijuana, and the number of indoor grow sites seized in Florida rose each year between 2004 (246 sites) and 2008 (1,022 sites). (See Table 6.)

Table 6. Number of Indoor Grow Sites and Plants Eradicated in Florida, 2004–2008.

	2004	2005	2006	2007	2008
Grow Sites	246	384	480	944	1,022
Plants	21,879	45,217	36,172	74,698	78,489

Source: Domestic Cannabis Eradication/Suppression Program.

MDMA Availability

Asian DTOs are responsible for a resurgence in MDMA availability in the United States, particularly since 2005. These groups produce large quantities of the drug in Canada and smuggle it into the United States across the Northern Border. The smuggling of MDMA into the United States from Canada fueled an increase in the availability of the drug that began in 2005, although availability appears to be stabilizing. Data regarding MDMA availability are limited; nonetheless, analysis of National Forensic Laboratory Information System (NFLIS) data shows a 76 percent increase in the number of MDMA submissions from 2005 to 2008 (see Figure 16), although MDMA submissions make up a much smaller percentage of submissions than other illicit drugs, including cannabis, cocaine, methamphetamine, and heroin. National Drug Threa National estimate (numbe of tota Survey (NDTS) data also provide an indication of MDMA availability. The percentage of state and local law enforcement agencies that reported moderate or high availability of MDMA in their areas increased from 47.2 percent in 2005 to 51.5 percent in 2009.

Seizure data show that the amount of MDMA seized along the U.S.–Canada border increased 156 percent from 2007 to 2008 (see Figure 17 on page 41) and that more MDMA was seized at the Northern Border in 2008 than in any year since 2005. MDMA seizure totals declined in 2009 but still exceeded 2007 totals.

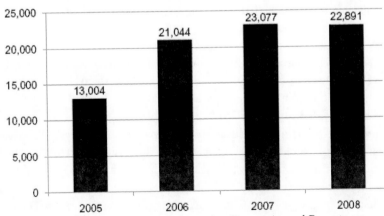

Source: National Forensic Laboratory Information System Annual Reports.

Figure 16. Number of MDMA Submissions, 2005–2008.

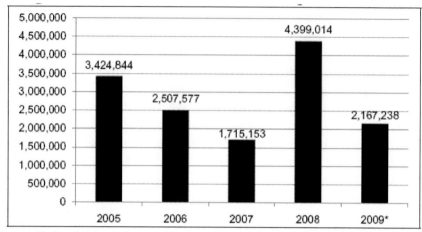

Source: National Seizure System. *Data as of December 1, 2009.

Figure 17. Northern Border MDMA Seizures, in Dosage Units, 2005–2009*.

Although most Northern Border seizures occur at POEs, the amount of MDMA seized between POEs appears to be increasing, likely because increased scrutiny at POEs has forced smugglers to develop new routes and smuggling methods in an attempt to circumvent law enforcement. For example, in 2008, more than 243,000 dosage units[18] of MDMA were seized between POEs, compared with none the previous year; seizures lyzed drug) between POEs in 2009 exceeded those in 2008.

MDMA seizures along the Southwest Border and through commercial air have also increased, albeit on a much smaller scale. Seizures at or near the Southwest Border show an increase from 114,286 dosage units in 2006 to 387,143 dosage units in 2009. Furthermore, commercial air seizures spiked in 2008, with a 91.4 percent increase from 2007 to 2008 (433,571 dosage units to 829,857 dosage units); MDMA commercial air seizure totals for 2009 decreased, resulting in levels comparable to 2007 levels.

Ready availability of MDMA has enabled distributors to expand their customer base to include new user groups, most notably African American and Hispanic users. Asian DTOs have begun distributing MDMA to African American and Hispanic street gangs, which distribute the drug along with other illicit drugs in markets throughout the United States, most notably in the Southeast, Southwest, and Great Lakes Regions. Moreover, MDMA is no longer exclusively viewed as a "rave" or club drug, which also aids distributors in selling it to nontraditional abusers.

CONTROLLED PRESCRIPTION DRUGS

The threat posed by the diversion and abuse of CPDs is increasing, largely aided by rapidly increasing distribution of the most addictive CPDs, prescription opioids (see text box). According to DEA, the amount of prescription opioids distributed to retail registrants increased 52 percent from 2003 through 2007.[19]

Prescription opioid overdose deaths are increasing, primarily because the decedents took the drugs nonmedically,[20] other than as prescribed, or in combination with other drugs and/or alcohol.

The number of unintentional prescription opioid overdose deaths increased in 2006,[21] following a trend that has been apparent since 2000. The overall rate of change from 2002 (5,547 deaths) through 2006[22] (11,001 deaths) was 98 percent, and the annual rate of change increased during that period (see Figure 18).

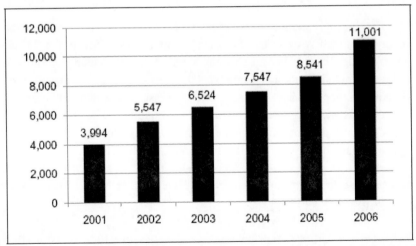

Source: Centers for Disease Control and Prevention, National Center for Health Statistics.

Figure 18. Number of Reported Unintentional Poisoning Deaths With Mention of Opioid Analgesics, 2001–2006.

Overdose death data do not provide in-depth information about the decedent's history of drug use or misuse or, in many cases, whether the decedent had a legitimate prescription for the drugs found in his or her system at the time of death. However, CDC reports that a high percentage of people who die from a prescription opioid poisoning have a history of substance abuse and that many have more than one CPD in their system at the time of death. For example, a 2008 CDC study found that 82.3 percent of diversion-related unintentional overdose decedents in West Virginia in 2006 had a history of substance abuse and that 79.3 percent had used multiple substances that contributed to their deaths. In many instances, these individuals were simply using prescription opioids (either singularly or in combination with other CPDs, alcohol, or illicit drugs) to achieve a heroin-like euphoria, and many did not have a legitimate prescription for the drugs. For example, the CDC study found that 63.1 percent of all unintentional CPD overdose deaths in West Virginia in 2006 involved individuals who did not have prescriptions for the drugs that contributed to their deaths.

PRESCRIPTION OPIOIDS

The most commonly diverted CPDs are opioid pain relievers, according to DEA and NSDUH data. Opioid pain relievers are popular among drug abusers because of the euphoria they induce. Opioid pain relievers include codeine, fentanyl (Duragesic, Actiq), hydromorphone (Dilaudid), meperidine (Demerol, which is prescribed less often because of its side effects), morphine (MS Contin), oxycodone (OxyContin), pentazocine (Talwin), dextropropoxyphene (Darvon), methadone (Dolophine), and hydrocodone combinations (Vicodin, Lortab, and Lorcet).

Source: Drug Enforcement Administration; Substance Abuse and Mental Health Services Administration.

More law enforcement agencies are reporting that pharmaceutical diversion and abuse pose the greatest drug threat to their areas, in part because of increases in associated crime and gang involvement, which put additional strain on agency budgets and assets.

A higher percentage of law enforcement agencies in all nine OCDETF regions responding to the NDTS 2009 reported diverted pharmaceuticals as their greatest drug threat in 2009 than they did in 2008 (see Figure 19). Law enforcement officers base their assessment of the threat on several factors, two of which are diversion- and abuse-related crime rates and gang involvement in drug distribution. For both of these factors, a higher percentage of agencies reported an increase in 2009 (see Table 7). The percentage of agencies reporting that pharmaceutical diversion and abuse contribute to other crime in their areas trended upward in seven of the nine OCDETF regions in 2009 (see Figure 20). The percentage of agencies reporting street gang involvement in pharmaceutical distribution also trended upward in six of the nine OCDETF regions in 2009 (see Figure 21 on page 45).

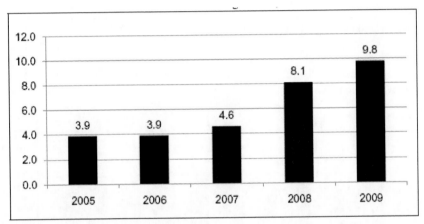

Source: National Drug Threat Survey 2009.

Figure 19. Percentage of State and Local Law Enforcement Agencies Reporting CPDs as Their Greatest Drug Threat, 2005–2009.

Table 7. Percentage of State and Local Law Enforcement Agencies Reporting Street Gang Involvement in Pharmaceutical Distribution and an Association an Between Pharmaceutical Diversion and Crime, 2008–2009.

	2008	2009
Street Gang Involvement	44.2%	48.0%
Property Crime	6.0%	8.4%
Violent Crime	3.5%	4.8%

Source: National Drug Threat Survey.

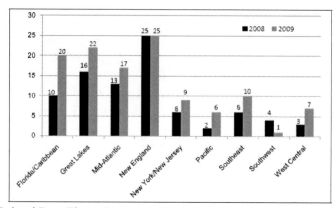

Source: National Drug Threat Survey.

Figure 20. Percentage of State and Local Law Enforcement Agencies Reporting an Association Between Pharmaceutical Diversion and Violent and Property Crimes by OCDETF Region, 2008–2009.

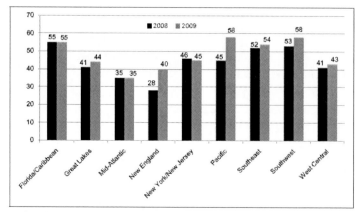

Source: National Drug Threat Survey.

Figure 21. Percentage of State and Local Law Enforcement Agencies Reporting Street Gang Involvement in Pharmaceutical Distribution, by OCDETF Region, 2008–2009.

Unscrupulous pain clinic physicians in Florida dispense or prescribe large quantities of prescription opioids to dealers and abusers and are a source of supply for opioids distributed in numerous states that have PDMPs.

Nonmedical personnel, primarily investors, are operating numerous purported pain clinics[23] in Broward and Palm Beach Counties, Florida. A

Florida grand jury found that from 2007 through 2009, the number of pain clinics in those counties grew from 4 to 115, and in one 6-month span, these pain clinic doctors dispensed more than 9 million tablets of oxycodone. The grand jury also found that the Broward and Palm Beach County clinics attract drug seekers from Kentucky, Ohio, Tennessee, and West Virginia.

Unscrupulous physicians—some with criminal records—employed at Florida clinics supply the constant demand for prescription opioids among distributors and abusers in Florida as well as among individuals from states in the Great Lakes, Mid-Atlantic, New England, and Southeast OCDETF Regions, where operational PDMPs have made acquiring CPDs more difficult. These physicians dispense or prescribe large quantities of prescription opioids to customers who have no legitimate need for the drugs; the physicians usually charge an up-front fee for this service and accept only cash payments. Florida law limited what regulators could do with regard to closing clinics or disciplining investors. For example, the Department of Health regulated healthcare professionals but not facilities; the Agency for Health Care Administration provided oversight on clinics that accept insurance, but illegal clinics usually accept only cash. Enacted in July 2009, Florida's new law establishing a PDMP requires that pain management clinics register with the Department of Health. Moreover, under the law, the state medical and osteopathic medicine boards must set standards of practice for all physicians and osteopaths who prescribe controlled substances from those clinics.

RECENT CASES INVOLVING THE UNLAWFUL DISPENSING OF CPDS

A Freeport, Florida, physician was sentenced in January 2009 to 292 months in prison and fined $250,000 after he was found guilty of 43 charges, including healthcare fraud; dispensing controlled substances, including fentanyl, hydrocodone, diazepam, clonazepam, morphine, and alprazolam, the use of which resulted in the death of two persons; and unlawfully dispensing controlled substances, including oxycodone, morphine, fentanyl, hydrocodone, alprazolam, diazepam, clonazepam, and carisoprodol. He also forfeited $260,000 in cash and his medical building for a total civil forfeiture of more than $835,000. The physician had owned and operated a clinic and prescribed CPDs to patients in quantities that made abuse and misuse likely. The physician failed to determine a sufficient medical necessity for the prescribing of these substances. Evi dence suggested that he had prescribed controlled substances to patients from across the southeastern United States, knowing that the patients were addicted to the substances, were misusing them, or were doctor-shopping.

The manager of two Florida pain management clinics and three prescribing physicians were sentenced in April 2009 for their roles in a prescription drug conspiracy. The manager was sentenced to 240 months in prison; one physician was sentenced to 30 months in prison, and the other two were sentenced to 72 months in prison. The manager of the clinic and the three physicians had purported to provide pain management treatment for chronic pain patients; however, they engaged in a conspiracy to unlawfully dispense hundreds of thousands of controlled pain medications, including OxyContin, Dilaudid, Roxicodone, oxycodone, Lortab, methadone, and others in exchange for cash fees for office visits. The manager was also convicted of possessing, carrying, and using a firearm in the furtherance of the conspiracy.

Federal law enforcement authorities in November 2009 dismantled a Florida trafficking ring that had sent more than 190,000 oxycodone tablets from South Florida pain clinics to abusers in Kentucky, North Carolina, Tennessee, Virginia, and West Virginia. At least 20 people were indicted on distribution charges; the ring had allegedly operated for 3 years and used at least four or five clinic doctors per day to obtain the drugs. Members of the ring shipped thousands of pills per day by vehicle or overnight delivery services and allegedly made at least $5 million over the 3 years.

Kentucky State Police detectives and troopers along with FBI agents, armed with 518 felony arrest warrants, conducted a drug roundup in October 2009 that stemmed from Operation Flamingo Road. This investigation targeted Kentucky drug traffickers in at least 33 counties who had traveled to South Florida to obtain CPDs from pain clinic doctors and returned to Kentucky to distribute the drugs. Penalties for felony charges of trafficking in controlled substances range from 18 months to 20 years in prison.

ILLICIT FINANCE

Tens of billions of dollars are laundered each year by drug traffickers operating in the United States. There are no current estimates for the annual amount of money either laundered domestically or smuggled out of the United States by DTOs. However, a 2007 NDIC study shows that from 2003 through 2004, at least $17.2 billion was smuggled into Mexico in bulk cash shipments alone.[24] Additionally, drug proceeds (perhaps totaling several billion dollars) are laundered each year through various techniques such as the use of the Black Market Peso Exchange (BMPE), money transmissions, front companies, real estate transactions, and structured deposits in traditional depository institutions. Because the predominant techniques used by DTOs to launder illicit drug proceeds have proved relatively successful, DTOs continue to rely on these methods to launder illicit drug proceeds. Nevertheless, there are some emerging developments related to money laundering.

Mexican DTOs smuggle bulk cash totaling tens of billions of dollars from specific domestic cash consolidation areas to and through POEs for eventual placement into foreign financial institutions.

Since 2001, enhanced U.S. anti-money laundering (AML) regulations such as the USA PATRIOT Act and law enforcement actions have made it more difficult to place drug proceeds into U.S. financial institutions. As a result, Mexican and, to a lesser extent, Canadian and other DTOs have adapted by smuggling bulk cash from drug sales out of the United States to countries where placement of the cash into financial institutions is much easier. In fact, bulk cash smuggling has become the primary method used by Mexican DTOs to move their U.S. drug proceeds. The exact amount of bulk cash smuggled out of the country by DTOs is unknown; however, it is at least tens of billions of dollars annually.

The movement of bulk cash by Mexican DTOs from U.S. drug markets, through key consolidation areas, to Mexico is a complex nationwide system. Millions of dollars in bulk cash is transported each week from U.S. drug markets to relatively few consolidation areas such as Atlanta, Chicago, Los Angeles, New York City, and North Carolina, where a Mexican DTO bulk cash cell leader takes direct control of the money. These drug proceeds are subsequently shipped to or across the Southwest Border. For example, law enforcement reporting and seizure data indicate that the volume of illicit bulk cash transported to and from Atlanta far exceeds that of any other city in the eastern half of the United States. In fact, the amount of cash seized from 2006 through June 2009 that was destined for Atlanta exceeded the amount destined for any other U.S. city outside the Southwest Border during that period. Mexican DTOs are the predominant drug traffickers in the Atlanta area, where they are able to coordinate large drug and money shipments. Because Atlanta is between major eastern drug markets and the Southwest Border, bulk cash is transported to stash houses in Atlanta, as well as a number of counties in northern Georgia, from across the southeastern United States and from as far away as New York City. As a result of increased law enforcement scrutiny, bulk cash consolidation operations have shifted from some of these major drug market areas into more rural areas or regional drug markets.

Canada-based DTOs smuggle bulk cash drug proceeds from the United States into Canada, often through remote areas of the U.S.– Canada border.

Canadian DTOs smuggle significant amounts of cash generated from the U.S. distribution of Canada-produced drugs into Canada. The Akwesasne Territory, which straddles the U.S.–Canada border, is one of the most important smuggling corridors for Canada-bound bulk cash. Overall, the topography of the U.S.–Canada border facilitates bulk cash smuggling because currency interdiction by law enforcement officials is often hampered by the border's length and vast expanses of rugged terrain.

The loss of Hong Kong Shanghai Banking Corporation (HSBC) Mexico for the placement of licit and illicit U.S. currency has had no long-term effect on BMPE placement activity in Mexico, since money launderers have repeatedly demonstrated their ability to quickly adapt to actions on the part of law enforcement and financial institutions.

The January 2009 implementation of the new HSBC Mexico AML policy, which stopped the deposit and exchange of foreign currency, has had no long-term effects on U.S. currency placement activity in Mexico. Drug proceeds in the form of bulk cash continue to be smuggled from domestic drug market areas to and across the U.S.–Mexico border as a principal placement method for BMPE transactions. Launderers operating in Mexico on behalf of BMPE peso brokers most likely have placed U.S. currency at Mexican financial institutions other than HSBC Mexico.

The potential for increased drug money laundering through the use of prepaid cards has prompted Nevada to enact state law SB-82 to aid law enforcement investigations involving this method of money laundering.

Prepaid card investigations and prosecutions are challenging because law enforcement officials must often secure warrants before accessing prepaid card account information, such as account balances and transaction records, or seizing funds stored on prepaid cards. As a result, law enforcement agents cannot efficiently determine whether the total value associated with a card is suspicious. It is also difficult for law enforcement officials to seize funds stored on prepaid cards, because those funds can be removed from the card by the criminal or a coconspirator while the card is in the possession of a law enforcement agency and before a seizure warrant can be obtained and executed.

Officials in Nevada have attempted to address these challenges with SB-82, which took effect July 1, 2009. This law makes it easier for Nevada law enforcement officials to investigate prepaid card money laundering and fraud cases that occur in the state each year. For example, SB-82 allows Nevada law enforcement to freeze the funds on a prepaid card for up to 10 days, until a judge authorizes a warrant, to prevent criminals from removing the funds while the card is in the possession of law enforcement authorities. In limited circumstances, SB-82 authorizes the seizure of funds without a warrant.

Changes to SWIFT[25] Message Format MT 202 will reduce money launderers' ability to disguise the origin and destination of wire transfers when wiring money through intermediary accounts.

Until recently, drug money launderers were able to take advantage of a vulnerability that existed in the wiring of money between banks without a direct banking relationship. When a bank needs to wire a customer's money to another bank, one of the several types of SWIFT messages may be used as instructions for the transfer. This message is sent through SWIFT separately from the actual settlement of the funds. When a customer's bank does not have a direct relationship with the ultimate receiving bank (a situation that occurs frequently, especially in international transfers), banks may use either cover payments[26] or serial payments[27] to send the money through one or more intermediate banks.[28]

In cases where cover payments are used, two separate SWIFT message instructions are sent. The first set of instructions, called MT 103, contains all of the originating customer and ultimate beneficiary information, but is seen only by the originating bank and the beneficiary bank. A second message, the MT 202, is sent to the intermediary banks. Previously, the SWIFT MT 202 messages that accompanied cover payments between intermediary banks did not retain originator and beneficiary account information.

This lack of information allowed money launderers to disguise their identity by sending wire transfers through intermediary banks. When a SWIFT 202 was used, only the originating and beneficiary bank, which could be foreign-based banks, could see the originator and beneficiary information. The intermediary banks, which would typically be U.S. banks, would not know this information.

This money laundering vulnerability has been eliminated by the new SWIFT Message Format, called MT 202 COV, which took effect November 21, 2009. The new format retains both originator and beneficiary information on all transfers made through intermediary banks, allowing intermediary banks to better investigate or block suspicious transactions.

The recent acquisition of a banking license by a virtual world company (online role- playing game) offers drug money launderers the ability to access the global financial system anonymously; however, large-scale use of virtual world banks to launder drug money is unlikely, since launderers remain encumbered by placement of drug proceeds.

In March 2009, a virtual world company (see following text box) received a license from the Swedish Financial Authority to conduct banking activities. This license enables the game's virtual economy to interact with and carry out the functions of real-world banks, such as offering interest-bearing savings, Automated Clearing House (ACH) transactions, and lending.[29] The ability to anonymously access the international financial system through this virtual world's bank creates a money laundering threat, particularly because rigorous know-your-customer procedures will be difficult to enforce. In virtual environments, role-playing games are built around the premise of players pretending to be other people. Establishing the actual identity of players will be very challenging for financial institutions and law enforcement.

WHAT IS A VIRTUAL WORLD?

Virtual worlds, also referred to as Massively Multiplayer Online Role-Playing Games, are Internet-based computer games characterized by a player assuming the role of a fictional character within the game, customizing that character, and interacting with other players of the game. Most games involve players cooperating with other players to complete tasks or quests in order to develop and advance their characters. However, some games are based around social interaction and have few, if any, specific tasks to complete or ways to advance character development.

Many online games have some form of in-game economy that allows players to buy and trade virtual items within the game. A few games let players transfer real-world money into and out of the virtual world, usually by means of credit card payments. This function has allowed players to start businesses in the virtual world and to transfer the profits out of the game to the real world.

Although there is a risk of abuse by drug money launderers, that risk is somewhat lessened because this virtual world bank will be subject to the same regulations and AML controls as real world banks. The usefulness of this virtual world's bank to money launderers also is limited by the need to first place cash into the financial system and the size of the online economy. In 2008, this game's economy was about $420 million generated from 820,000 players. Typically, users spend between $.50 and $1.50 per hour in the game. Large or very frequent transactions would stand out from normal players' transactions.

A U.S. Supreme Court decision that differentiates between bulk cash smuggling and money laundering will likely inhibit future money laundering prosecutions of bulk cash couriers.

On June 1, 2008, the Supreme Court ruled that a suspected bulk cash courier who was arrested while transporting $81,000 to Mexico in the hidden compartment of a passenger vehicle was not guilty of money laundering. The decision establishes a separation between bulk cash smuggling and money laundering. In the ruling, the court wrote, "Although the evidence showed intent to avoid detection while driving the money to Mexico, it did not show that the petitioner intended to create the appearance of legitimate wealth, and accordingly no rational trier of fact could have found the petitioner guilty."

The ruling will most likely limit prosecutions against bulk cash smugglers; therefore, bulk cash smuggling in the United States will likely continue unabated. Despite this ruling, DTO leaders are unlikely to challenge bulk cash seizures or arrests for fear of exposing their financial infrastructures through legal proceedings. Currently, most couriers who are stopped during suspected drug cash interdictions deny knowledge of the cash and are released, at which point law enforcement officials are able to seize the currency.

VULNERABILITIES

Large-scale methamphetamine production is very dependent on a consistent supply of bulk precursor chemicals such as ephedrine, pseudoephedrine, and P2P. Such supplies are available from companies producing the chemicals in relatively few countries, including China and India. Increased cooperation from these countries and the companies producing the chemicals could greatly disrupt methamphetamine production and availability.

Drug shipments entering the United States are vulnerable to detection and interdiction at POEs. Wholesale seizures at POEs are typically larger than seizures in the interior of the country because loads have not been divided for midlevel or retail distribution. However, DTOs employ spotters to closely monitor the flow of traffic through POEs. These spotters direct load vehicles in real time to specific lanes that they believe will have the highest chance for successful entry into the United States without inspection. Denying spotters clear visibility of the POE lanes through the use of lights or visual barriers would reduce the success of smugglers. Alternatively, implementing a process that would randomly direct vehicles to specific lanes would also deny spotters any advantage.

Seizures of illicit drugs from stash sites along the Southwest Border region result in a much greater loss to Mexican DTOs than seizures that take place after the drugs have been broken into smaller shipments for distribution in retail drug markets. Identifying load vehicles at POEs and then conducting controlled deliveries or simply tracking them to Southwest Border stash sites might be an effective method of detecting such sites and increasing drug seizures.

Domestic drug transportation in commercial tractor-trailers is vulnerable to highway interdiction. Because tractor-trailers typically travel interstates or larger U.S. highways to transport large drug shipments to domestic drug markets, nationally coordinated domestic surge operations to bring about intense and sustained interdiction efforts could increase the amount of drugs seized domestically.

The activities of Mexican DTOs are particularly vulnerable to detection when they attempt to expand drug distribution into new markets. When DTOs expand into new drug markets, they often lack a reliable network of distributors and security personnel in those new markets. As a result, they are more likely to deal with new, unproven local dealers, rendering the organization vulnerable to undercover law enforcement operations.

Highly addictive prescription opioids are primarily acquired by users through doctor- shopping. In states that have implemented comprehensive PDMPs,[30] doctor-shopping has decreased. However, many individuals continue to acquire the drugs by simply travelling to doctors in nearby states where there are no such programs. State PDMPs that require nationwide data sharing would curtail the practice of traveling to neighboring states for prescription opioids and would most likely reduce doctor-shopping significantly.

Many prescription drug abusers, especially younger abusers, acquire CPDs through theft from family members or acquaintances who have legitimate prescriptions for the drugs. Often these drugs are unused and unneeded pills prescribed to treat pain for a temporary condition such as recovery from a surgery. Implementing a national incentive program for patients to return unused pills to collection facilities for proper disposal would reduce the diversion and misuse of CPDs (see text box on page 52).

Bulk cash shipments of illicit drug proceeds are at risk of seizure at stash houses in consolidation cities and in transit to and across the Southwest Border. DTOs have developed elaborate countermeasures to minimize this risk, such as choosing unassuming locations, limiting the number of individuals who have knowledge of the stash house sites, and moving bulk cash quickly through stash houses. However, a dedicated investigative team capable of developing and exploiting organizational intelligence in each of the leading bulk cash consolidation cities could result in significant bulk cash seizures in those cities. Moreover, enhanced interdiction efforts and rigorous outbound inspections of vehicles leaving the United States would very likely result in a sharp increase in bulk cash seizures.

PRESCRIPTION DRUG DISPOSAL PROGRAMS

Concerns regarding drug diversion and environmental pollution resulting from uncontrolled disposal prompted a flurry of activity at the state, local, and federal levels in 2009. Many state and local law enforcement agencies followed Florida law enforcement's lead by conducting medicine take-back programs. Through these programs, people with leftover medications were encouraged to turn them in to law enforcement officers at specific locations. The take-back programs resulted in the collection of tens of thousands of pounds of prescription drugs. Broward County, Florida, law enforcement officers held the first Operation Medicine Cabinet (OMC) program in 2008. Since then, OMC programs have become increasingly popular and have been held in states such as Georgia, Indiana, Iowa, and New Jersey. Other states have held take-back programs similar to OMC using various names for the programs. Maine established a year-round take-back program using the mail service. The majority of drugs collected at all take-back events are noncontrolled substances, but many of the drugs are CPDs. Quantities of prescription drugs turned in during take-back events include the following:

- Great Lakes, Earth Day 2009: 4 million pills
- Illinois, 2008–2009: 90,000+ pounds of pills
- Iowa, 2008: 1,029 pounds
- Maine, 2009: 2,123 pounds noncontrolled and 252 pounds CPDs
- Michigan, 2009: 6,866 noncontrolled pills and 1,483 CPDs (2-week span)
- New Jersey, 2009: 9,000 pounds (3.5 million pills)
- Salisbury, North Carolina, 2009: 157 pounds
- Washington State, 2006–2009: 11,000 pounds
- Watauga County, North Carolina, 2009: 40,000 pills, 12 gallons of liquid medication

Under the Controlled Substances Act (CSA), ultimate users[a] do not have DEA registration numbers permitting them to distribute controlled substances; therefore, users are not permitted to distribute unused drugs even to those officers conducting take-back programs. However, it was determined that current take-back programs could use an exemption from registration that permits law enforcement officers to handle controlled drugs while acting in an official capacity. In early 2009, the DEA Office of Diversion Control began to seek comments on options to CSA amendments addressing individual disposal of patient-owned controlled substances. To amend the CSA, DEA is awaiting congressional action on several related pieces of legislation.

At the federal level, several bills (HR 1191 and companion SB 1336, and HR 1359 and companion SB 1292) were introduced in the House of Representatives in 2009 to amend the *CSA*. HR 1191 provides for disposal of CPDs through state take-back programs, while HR 1359 permits the consumer to deliver drugs for disposal. HR 1191 also recommended amending the Food, Drug, and Cosmetic Act to prohibit product labeling that proposed flushing of unused prescription drugs. Both bills were referred to the House Committee on Energy and Commerce and the House Committee on the Judiciary in 2009. DOJ has endorsed HR 1359 and SB 1292, since they afford the most flexibility.

At the state level, legislators in Florida, Maine, Minnesota, Oregon, and Washington introduced bills in 2009 that would require drug manufacturers to operate and pay for systems that facilitate the collection, transportation, and disposal of leftover prescription drugs. In California, a senate bill was being considered in 2009 that would require the state's Board of Pharmacy to work with other state agencies, local governments, drug manufacturers, and pharmacies to develop sustainable programs to manage the disposal of prescription drugs.

a. The CSA defines an "ultimate user" as a person who obtains a drug legally and possesses it for his or her own use, for a family member's use, or for use in an animal in the household.

OUTLOOK

The growing strength and organization of criminal gangs, including their growing alliances with large Mexican DTOs, has changed the nature of midlevel and retail drug distribution in many local drug markets, even in suburban and rural areas. As a result, disrupting illicit drug availability and distribution will become increasingly difficult for state and local law enforcement agencies. In many of these markets, local independent dealers can no longer compete with national-level gangs that can undersell local drug distributors. Previously, state and local law enforcement agencies could disrupt drug availability in their areas, at least temporarily, by investigating and dismantling local distribution groups. But well-organized criminal gangs are able to maintain a stronger, more stable drug supply to local markets and to quickly replace distributors when individual gang members or entire distribution cells are arrested. Significantly disrupting drug distribution in smaller drug markets will increasingly require large-scale multijurisdictional investigations, most likely necessitating federal law enforcement support.

Without a significant increase in drug interdiction, seizures, arrests, and investigations that apply sustained pressure on major DTOs, availability of most drugs will increase in 2010, primarily because drug production in Mexico is increasing. The most recent drug production estimates show sharp increases in heroin and marijuana production in Mexico and greatly reduced efforts to eradicate drug crops in that country. The production estimates are supported by Southwest Border drug seizure data showing sharp increases in heroin and marijuana seizures in 2009. Southwest Border seizure data also indicate that methamphetamine production has increased sharply in Mexico as well because of traffickers' ability to circumvent precursor chemical restrictions and employ alternative production methods despite strong GOM restrictions on ephedrine and pseudoephedrine imports. Only cocaine production estimates show decreasing production in Colombia, and that trend is reflected in availability data, including cocaine seizure data, which show relatively low availability of the drug.

The increased enforcement against illegal pain clinics and the growing number of PDMPs will increasingly disrupt the supply of CPDs to prescription opioid users who typically acquire these drugs through doctor- shopping and from unscrupulous physicians. Many users will seek CPDs from other sources, including pharmacy robberies. The number of pharmacy armed robberies has increased over the past 5 years, and in many states, laws are not sufficient to deter such crimes. Other prescription opioid users will increasingly switch to heroin because, according to reporting from law enforcement and treatment providers, in many instances heroin is less expensive than diverted prescription opioids.

APPENDIX A. MAPS

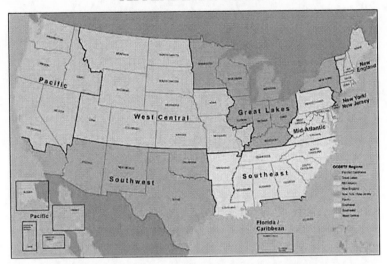

Map A1. Nine OCDETF Regions.

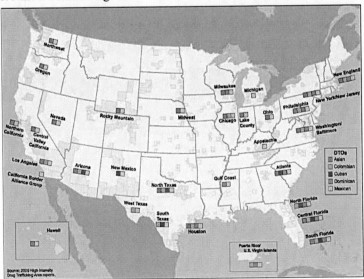

*Map depicts presence only, not level of activity.

Map A2. Drug Distribution by Select DTOs, by HIDTA Region*.

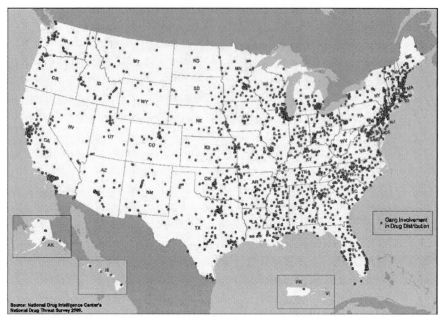

Source: National Drug Intelligence Center's National Drug Threat Survey 2009.

Map A3. 2009 Street Gang Involvement in Drug Distribution.

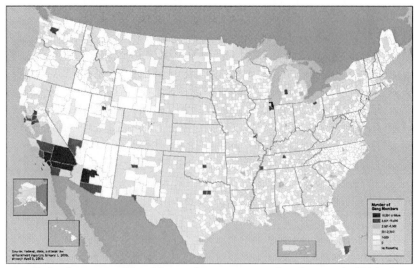

Source: Federal, state, and local law enforcement reporting January 1, 2006, through April 8, 2008.

Map A4. Gang Membership by County.

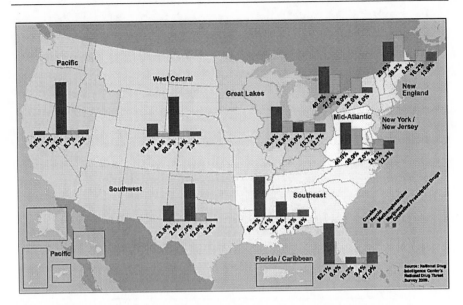

Map A5. 2009 Greatest Drug Threat by Region, as Reported by State and Local Agencies.

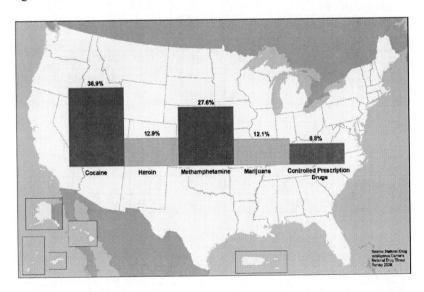

Map A6. 2009 Greatest Drug Threat, as Reported by State and Local Agencies.

APPENDIX B. TABLES

Table B1. Trends in Percentage of Past Year Drug Use, 2004–2008.

Drug	2004	2005	2006	2007	2008
Cocaine (any form)					
Individuals (12 and older)	2.4	2.3	2.5	2.3	2.1
Adolescents (12-17)	1.6	1.7	1.6	1.5	1.2
Adults (18-25)	6.6	6.9	6.9	6.4	5.5
Adults (26 and older)	1.7	1.5	1.8	1.7	1.6
Crack					
Individuals (12 and older)	0.5	0.6	0.6	0.6	0.4
Adolescents (12-17)	0.3	0.2	0.3	0.3	0.1
Adults (18-25)	0.8	1.0	0.9	0.8	0.6
Adults (26 and older)	0.5	0.5	0.6	0.6	0.4
Heroin					
Individuals (12 and older)	0.2	0.2	0.2	0.1	0.2
Adolescents (12-17)	0.2	0.1	0.1	0.1	0.2
Adults (18-25)	0.4	0.5	0.4	0.4	0.4
Adults (26 and older)	0.1	0.1	0.2	0.1	0.1
Marijuana					
Individuals (12 and older)	10.6	10.4	10.3	10.1	10.3
Adolescents (12-17)	14.5	13.3	13.2	12.5	13.0
Adults (18-25)	27.8	28.0	28.0	27.5	27.6
Adults (26 and older)	7.0	6.9	6.8	6.8	7.0
Methamphetamine					
Individuals (12 and older)	0.8	0.7	0.8	0.5	0.3
Adolescents (12-17)	0.7	0.7	0.7	0.5	0.4
Adults (18-25)	1.9	1.8	1.7	1.2	0.8
Adults (26 and older)	0.6	0.5	0.6	0.4	0.3
Prescription Narcotics					
Individuals (12 and older)	4.7	4.9	5.1	5.0	4.8
Adolescents (12-17)	7.4	6.9	7.2	6.7	6.5
Adults (18-25)	11.9	12.4	12.4	12.1	12.0
Adults (26 and older)	3.0	3.3	3.6	3.6	3.3

Table B1. (Continued)

Drug	2004	2005	2006	2007	2008
LSD					
Individuals (12 and older)	0.2	0.2	0.3	0.3	0.3
Adolescents (12-17)	0.6	0.6	0.4	0.5	0.7
Adults (18-25)	1.0	1.0	1.2	1.1	1.5
Adults (26 and older)	0.1	0.0	0.1	0.1	0.1
MDMA					
Individuals (12 and older)	0.8	0.8	0.9	0.9	0.9
Adolescents (12-17)	1.2	1.0	1.2	1.3	1.4
Adults (18-25)	3.1	3.1	3.8	3.5	3.9
Adults (26 and older)	0.3	0.4	0.3	0.3	0.3
PCP					
Individuals (12 and older)	0.1	0.1	0.1	0.1	0.0
Adolescents (12-17)	0.3	0.3	0.2	0.2	0.2
Adults (18-25)	0.3	0.2	0.2	0.2	0.1
Adults (26 and older)	0.0	0.0	0.0	0.0	*

Source: National Survey on Drug Use and Health.
*Low precision; no estimate reported.

Table B2. Admissions to Publicly Funded Treatment Facilities by Primary Substance, 2003–2007.

Drug	2003	2004	2005	2006	2007
Cocaine	254,687	249,478	266,420	262,720	234,772
Heroin	273,996	261,610	259,462	264,599	246,871
Marijuana	291,470	287,121	301,263	299,692	287,933
Methamphetamine	114,451	125,361	154,447	152,561	137,154
Barbiturates	1,337	1,303	1,380	1,046	1,013
Other opiates/synthetics	52,840	61,340	70,268	80,131	90,516
Tranquilizers	8,164	8,212	8,458	9,334	9,949

Source: Treatment Episode Data Set.

Table B3. Drugs Distribution in the United States, by DTOs and OCDETF Region.

OCDETF /DTO	Mexican	Asian	Colombian	Dominican	Cuban
Florida/ Caribbean	Cocaine Heroin Marijuana Methamphetamine	Marijuana MDMA	Cocaine Heroin	Cocaine Heroin Marijuana	Cocaine Heroin Marijuana
Great Lakes	Cocaine Heroin Marijuana Methamphetamine	Cocaine Heroin Marijuana MDMA	Cocaine Heroin	Cocaine Heroin	—
Mid-Atlantic	Cocaine Heroin Marijuana Methamphetamine	Marijuana MDMA	Cocaine Heroin	Cocaine Heroin Marijuana	—
New England	Cocaine Heroin Marijuana Methamphetamine	Marijuana MDMA Methamphetamine	Cocaine Heroin Marijuana	Cocaine Heroin Marijuana	—
New York/ New Jersey	Cocaine Heroin Marijuana MDMA Methamphetamine	Heroin Marijuana MDMA	Cocaine Heroin Marijuana	Cocaine Heroin Marijuana MDMA	—
Pacific	Cocaine Her-oin Marijuana Methamphetamine	Marijuana MDMA Methamphetamine	—	—	—
Southeast	Cocaine Heroin Marijuana Methamphetamine	Marijuana MDMA	—	Cocaine Marijuana	Marijuana
Southwest	Cocaine Heroin Marijuana Methamphetamine	Cocaine Marijuana MDMA Methamphetamine	Cocaine Heroin Marijuana Methamphetamine	Cocaine	Cocaine Marijuana Methamphetamine
West Central	Cocaine Heroin Marijuana Methamphetamine	Marijuana MDMA	—	—	—

Source: Federal, state, and local law enforcement reporting.

Table B4. Gangs with Significant Influence on U.S. Drug Markets.

Name	Primary Areas of Operation	Drugs Trafficked	Affiliations (DTOs)
18th Street	Pacific Southwest	Methamphetamine	Sinaloa Tijuana
Bandidos	Southwest Pacific	Cocaine Heroin Marijuana Methamphetamine	Juárez
Barrio Azteca	Southwest	Cocaine Heroin Marijuana Methamphetamine	Juárez
Black Guerilla Family	Pacific Mid-Atlantic	Cocaine Marijuana	Sinaloa
Bloods	New England New York/New Jersey Southeast Southwest Pacific	Cocaine Heroin Marijuana MDMA	Tijuana Sinaloa
Crips	New England Southeast Southwest Pacific	Cocaine Heroin Marijuana MDMA	Juárez
Florencia 13	Pacific Southwest Southeast	Cocaine Heroin Marijuana Methamphetamine	Tijuana Sinaloa
Gangster Disciples	Great Lakes Pacific Southeast West Central	Cocaine Heroin Marijuana	Sinaloa

Table B4. (Continued)

Name	Primary Areas of Operation	Drugs Trafficked	Affiliations (DTOs)
Hells Angels	Pacific Southwest New England New York/New Jersey	Cocaine Marijuana MDMA	Sinaloa Tijuana
Hermanos de Pistoleros Latinos	Southwest	Cocaine Marijuana	Gulf Coast Zetas
Latin Kings	Florida Great Lakes New England New York/New Jersey Mid-Atlantic Pacific Southeast Southwest West Central	Cocaine Heroin Marijuana MDMA	Juárez Sinaloa Gulf Coast
Ñeta	Southeast Mid-Atlantic New England New York/New Jersey	Cocaine Marijuana	Unknown
Mara Salvatrucha	Mid-Atlantic New England New York/New Jersey Southeast Southwest West Central Pacific	Cocaine Heroin Marijuana Methamphetamine	Sinaloa Gulf Coast Zetas
Mexican Mafia	Southwest Pacific	Cocaine Marijuana	Sinaloa Tijuana Zetas
Mexikanemi	Southwest	Cocaine Marijuana Methamphetamine	Gulf Coast Zetas
Norteños	Pacific Southwest	Cocaine Marijuana Methamphetamine	Sinaloa Tijuana
Sureños	Pacific Southwest West Central Southeast Southeast	Cocaine Heroin Marijuana Methamphetamine	Sinaloa Tijuana
Tango Blast	Southwest	Cocaine Marijuana	Gulf Coast Zetas

Table B4. (Continued)

Name	Primary Areas of Operation	Drugs Trafficked	Affiliations (DTOs)
Texas Syndicate	Southwest	Cocaine Marijuana	Gulf Coast Zetas
Tiny Rascal Gangsters	New England Pacific	Marijuana MDMA	Asian DTOs
Vagos	Pacific Southwest	Cocaine Marijuana	Tijuana

Source: United States Department of Justice, Attorney General's Report to Congress on Growth of Violent Street Gangs in Suburban Areas, April 2000; High Intensity Drug Trafficking Area reporting.

Table B5. Pseudoephedrine Scheduling by State.

State	Currently Schedules Pseudoephedrine	Currently Has Point-of-Sale Restrictions	Currently Has Pseudoephedrine Tracking Laws
AK	No	Quantity, Packaging	No
AL	No	Quantity, Packaging, Display/Offer	Yes
AR	Schedule V	Quantity, Packaging, Display/Offer	Yes
AZ	Schedule V	Quantity	In Legislature
CA	No	Quantity	No
CO	No	Packaging	No
CT	No	No	No
DC	No	No	No
DE	No	Quantity, Display/Offer	No
FL	No	Quantity, Display/Offer	Yes
GA	Exempt Schedule V	Quantity, Packaging	In Legislature
HI	No	Quantity, Packaging, Display/Offer	Yes
IA	Schedule V	Quantity, Display/Offer	Yes
ID	Schedule II	Display/Offer	No
IL	Schedule V	Quantity, Display/Offer	Yes

Table B5. (Continued)

State	Currently Schedules Pseudoephedrine	Currently Has Point-of-Sale Restrictions	Currently Has Pseudoephedrine Tracking Laws
IN	No	Quantity, Display/Offer	In Legislature
KS	Schedule V	Quantity, Packaging, Display/Offer	Yes
KY	No	Quantity	Yes
LA	Schedule V	Quantity, Display/Offer	Yes
MA	No	No	No
MD	No	No	In Legislature
ME	Maine designates its four schedules of controlled substances as W, X, Y, and Z. Pseudoephedrine is classified as Z.	Quantity, Packaging, and Display	No
MI	No	Quantity, Display/Offer	Yes
MN	Schedule V	Quantity, Packaging, Display/Offer	Yes
MO	Schedule V	Quantity, Display/Offer	Yes
MS	No	Quantity, Display/Offer	Yes
MT	No	Quantity, Display/Offer	No
NC	Schedule VI1	Quantity, Packaging, Display/Offer	Yes
ND	No	Quantity, Packaging, Display/Offer	Yes
NE	No	Quantity, Packaging, Display/Offer	No
NH	No	No	No
NJ	No	Quantity	No
NM	Schedule V	Quantity, Display/Offer	Yes

Table B5. (Continued)

State	Currently Schedules Pseudoephedrine	Currently Has Point-of-Sale Restrictions	Currently Has Pseudoephedrine Tracking Laws
NV	Schedule III2	No	No
NY	No	No	No
OH	No	Quantity, Display/Offer	Yes
OK	Schedule V	Quantity, Display/Offer	Yes
OR	Schedule III	No	No
PA	No	Quantity, Packaging, and Display	In Legislature
PR/ US VI	No	No	No
RI	No	Quantity	Yes
SC	No	Quantity, Packaging, Display/Offer	Yes
SD	No	Quantity, Packaging, Display/Offer	No
TN	Schedule V	Quantity, Packaging, Display/Offer	Yes
TX	No	Quantity, Display/Offer	Yes
UT	No	Quantity, Display/Offer	Yes
VA	No	Quantity, Display/Offer	In Legislature
VT	No	Quantity, Packaging, Display/Offer	No
WA	Schedule II3	Quantity, Packaging, Display/Offer	Yes
WI	Schedule V	Quantity	Yes
WV	Schedule V	Quantity, Display/Offer	Yes
WY	No	Quantity, Packaging, Display/Offer	No

1. NC Code 90-94.

2. Excludes drug products approved under federal law for over-the-counter sale.

3. Excludes "any drug or compound containing Pseudoephedrine... that [is] prepared for dispensing or over-the-counter distribution and [is] in compliance with the Federal Food, Drug and Cosmetic Act and applicable regulations."

APPENDIX C. SCOPE AND METHODOLOGY

The *National Drug Threat Assessment 2010* is a comprehensive assessment of the threat posed to the United States by the trafficking and abuse of illicit drugs. It was prepared through detailed analysis of the most recent law enforcement, intelligence, and public health data available to NDIC through the date of publication.

The *National Drug Threat Assessment 2010* includes information provided by 3,069 state and local law enforcement agencies through the NDIC National Drug Threat Survey 2009. State and local law enforcement agencies also provided information through personal interviews with NDIC Field Intelligence Officers (FIOs), a nationwide network of law enforcement professionals assembled by NDIC to promote information sharing among federal, state, and local law enforcement agencies.

This report addresses emerging developments related to the trafficking and use of primary illicit substances of abuse, the nonmedical use of CPDs, and the laundering of proceeds generated through illicit drug sales. It also addresses the role that DTOs and organized gangs play in domestic drug trafficking, the significant role that the Southwest Border plays in the illicit drug trade, and the societal impact of drug abuse. Analysts considered various quantitative data (data on seizures, investigations, arrests, drug purity or potency, and drug prices; law enforcement surveys; laboratory analyses; and interagency production and cultivation estimates) and qualitative information (subjective views of individual agencies on drug availability, information on the involvement of organized criminal groups, information on smuggling and transportation trends, and indicators of change in smuggling and transportation methods) in the preparation of this report.

The evaluation of societal impact was based in part on analysis of national substance abuse data measuring prevalence of drug use among various age groups, ED information, information on admissions to treatment facilities, and information on drug-related crimes. The societal impact of drugs was also evaluated through analysis of health care, criminal justice, workplace productivity, and environmental data and reporting.

NDTS data used in this report do not imply that there is only one drug threat per state or region or that only one drug is available per state or region. A percentage given for a state or region represents the proportion of state and local law enforcement agencies in that state or region that identified a particular drug as the greatest threat or as available at low, moderate, or high levels. This assessment breaks the country into nine regions as shown in Map

A1 in Appendix A. For representation of survey data by regions, see Map A5 in Appendix A. For national-level data, see Map A6 in Appendix A.

SOURCES

Numerous state and local law enforcement agencies throughout the United States provided valuable input to this report through their participation in the NDTS and interviews with NDIC FIOs. These agencies are too numerous to thank individually.

Central Intelligence Agency
  Crime And Narcotics Center
Executive Office of the President
  Office of National Drug Control Policy
    High Intensity Drug Trafficking Areas
      Appalachia
      Arizona
      Atlanta
      Central Florida
      Central Valley California
      Chicago
      Gulf Coast
      Hawaii
      Houston
      Lake County
      Los Angeles
      Michigan
      Midwest
      Milwaukee
      Nevada
      New England
      New York/New Jersey
      Northern California
      North Florida
      North Texas
      Northwest
      Ohio
      Oregon

Philadelphia/Camden
Puerto Rico/U.S. Virgin Islands
Rocky Mountain
South Florida
Southwest Border
Washington/Baltimore

Government of Mexico
Attorney General's Office
Center for Analysis, Planning, and Intelligence Against Organized Crime

Government of the United Kingdom
Home Office
Serious Organised Crime Agency

International Council of Securities Associations

National Alliance of Gang Investigators Associations

U.S. Department of Agriculture
Forest Service
National Forest System

U.S. Department of Commerce
U.S. Census Bureau

U.S. Department of Defense
Defense Intelligence Agency
U.S. Army
National Guard Bureau

U.S. Department of Health And Human Services
Centers for Disease Control and Prevention
National Institutes of Health
National Institute on Drug Abuse
Substance Abuse and Mental Health Services Administration
Drug Abuse Warning Network
National Survey on Drug Use and Health
Treatment Episode Data Set

U.S. Department of Homeland Security
U.S. Coast Guard
Maritime Intelligence Center
U.S. Customs and Border Protection
Border Patrol Intelligence Center
U.S. Immigration and Customs Enforcement

U.S. Department of Justice
  Bureau of Alcohol, Tobacco, Firearms and Explosives
  Bureau of Justice Assistance
  Middle Atlantic–Great Lakes Organized Crime Law Enforcement Network
  Mid-States Organized Crime Information Center New England State Police Information Network Regional Information Sharing Systems
  Regional Organized Crime Information Center Rocky Mountain Information Network
  Western States Information Network
  Criminal Division
  Organized Crime Drug Enforcement Task Force
  Drug Enforcement Administration
   Atlanta Division
   Boston Division
   Caribbean Division
   Chicago Division
   Cocaine Program
   Dallas Division
   Denver Division
   Detroit Division
   Domestic Cannabis Eradication/Suppression Program
   Domestic Monitor Program
   El Paso Division
   El Paso Intelligence Center
     National Seizure System
   Federal-Wide Drug Seizure System
   Heroin Domestic Monitor Program
   Heroin Signature Program
   Houston Division
   Los Angeles Division
   Miami Division
   National Forensic Laboratory Information System
   Newark Division
   New Orleans Division
   New York Division
   Office of Diversion Control
   Philadelphia Division
   Phoenix Division

    San Diego Division
    San Francisco Division
    Seattle Division
    Special Operations Division
    St. Louis Division
    System to Retrieve Information From Drug Evidence
    Washington, D.C., Division
Executive Office for U.S. Attorneys
  U.S. Attorneys Offices
Federal Bureau of Investigation
  Albany Field Office
  Albuquerque Field Office
  Anchorage Field Office
  Atlanta Field Office
  Baltimore Field Office
  Birmingham Field Office
  Boston Field Office
  Buffalo Field Office
  Charlotte Field Office
  Chicago Field Office
  Cincinnati Field Office
  Cleveland Field Office
  Columbia Field Office
  Dallas Field Office
  Denver Field Office
  Detroit Field Office
  El Paso Field Office
  Honolulu Field Office
  Houston Field Office
  Indianapolis Field Office
  Jackson Field Office
  Jacksonville Field Office
  Kansas City Field Office
  Knoxville Field Office
  Las Vegas Field Office
  Little Rock Field Office
  Los Angeles Field Office
  Louisville Field Office
  Memphis Field Office

Milwaukee Field Office
Minneapolis Field Office
Mobile Field Office
National Gang Intelligence Center
Newark Field Office
New Haven Field Office
New Orleans Field Office
New York Field Office
Norfolk Field Office
North Miami Beach Field Office
Oklahoma City Field Office
Omaha Field Office
Philadelphia Field Office
Phoenix Field Office
Pittsburgh Field Office
Portland Field Office
Richmond Field Office
Sacramento Field Office
Salt Lake City Field Office
San Antonio Field Office
San Diego Field Office
San Francisco Field Office
San Juan Field Office
Seattle Field Office
Springfield Field Office
St. Louis Field Office
Strategic Intelligence and Analysis Unit
Tampa Field Office
Washington, D.C., Field Office
National Institute of Justice
  Arrestee Drug Abuse Monitoring Program
Office of Justice Programs
  Bureau of Justice Statistics
U.S. Department of State
International Narcotics Control Strategy Report
U.S. Government Accountability Office
U.S. Postal Service
  U.S. Postal Inspection Service
U.S. Sentencing Commission

Other

American Medical Association
Drug Take-Back Network
National Crime Victimization Survey
National Parks Conservation Association
Product Stewardship Institute
Quest Diagnostics Incorporated
United Nations
University of Chicago
   National Opinion Research Center
University of San Diego
   Trans-Border Institute
World Health Organization

End Notes

[1] The findings presented in this assessment are based on exacting analysis of quantitative data sources (data on seizures, investigations, arrests, drug purity or potency, drug prices, law enforcement surveys, laboratory analyses, and interagency production and cultivation estimates) and qualitative information including subjective views by individual agencies on various drug-related issues (see Appendix C: Scope and Methodology on page 69). For in-depth analysis of key issues in this summary, refer to individual chapters in this document.

[2] Information based on a National Survey on Drug Use and Health (NSDUH) sample survey.

[3] Estimate is based on a 2002 Office of National Drug Control Policy (ONDCP) estimate of $180 billion that has been adjusted for inflation.

[4] Nonmedical use of prescription-type psychotherapeutics includes the nonmedical use of pain relievers, tranquilizers, stimulants, and sedatives but excludes over-the-counter drugs.

[5] DAWN defines drug-related deaths as deaths that are natural or accidental with drug involvement, deaths involving homicide by drug, and deaths with drug involvement when the manner of death denoted by the medical examiner is "could not be determined."

[6] Data include alcohol dependence or alcohol abuse.

[7] The research also included antibiotics, steroids, and more than 100 pharmaceuticals.

[8] National Seizure System data as of December 1, 2009.

[9] Includes incarcerated gang members.

[10] Rocking is defined as the throwing of rocks at Border Patrol agents by drug or alien smugglers with the intent of threatening or causing physical harm to the agent.

[11] Straw purchasers are intermediaries who acquire one or more firearms from a licensed firearms dealer on behalf of another person. The purpose is to hide the identity of the true purchaser or ultimate possessor of the firearm(s).

[12] Excludes cities within the Southwest Border Arrival Zone area (within 150 miles of the U.S.–Mexico border).

[13] Availability indicatorsvary by drug typeand include drug and laboratory seizure data, DAWN emergency department data, Quest Diagnostics workplace testing data, National Forensic Laboratory Information System (NFLIS) data, and DEA price andpurity data.

[14] Superlabs are laboratories capable of producing 10 or more pounds of methamphetamine in a single production cycle.

[15] Smurfing is a method used by some methamphetamine and precursor chemical traffickers to acquire large quantities of pseudoephedrine. Individuals purchase pseudoephedrine in quantities at or below legal thresholds from multiple retail locations. Traffickers often enlist the assistance of several associates in smurfing operations to increase the speed with which chemicals are acquired.

[16] No reliable estimates are available regardingthe amount ofdomestically cultivated or processed marijuana. The amountof marijuana available in theUnitedStates— including marijuana producedboth domestically and internationally—isunknown. Moreover, estimates as to the extent of domestic cannabis cultivation are not feasible because of significant variability in or nonexistence of dataregarding the number of cannabis plantsnot eradicated during eradication seasons, cannabis eradication effectiveness, and plant-yield estimates.

[17] Noestimatesareavailableregarding the amountof marijuana producedby Asian, Caucasian, Mexican, and Cubantraffickers in theUnitedStates;currently, no national-level eradication statistics are compiled or recorded by theproducing group.The lackof such estimates precludes a precise determination of the extent towhich each group is involved in marijuana production within the United States.

[18] MDMA tablets vary in size and weight depending on the manufacturing process, the type of pill press being used, and the amount of adulterants incorporated into the tablet. m Annual Reports Therefore a standard dosage unit of 140 milligrams per tablet is used to convert other units of measure, such as kilograms, for consistency and estimates on total dosage units.

[19] The narcotic raw material produced in or imported into the United States is subject to an annual assessment of legitimate medical, scientific, and research need and the establishment of quotas by DEA. Contributing factors to quota increases include: more aggressive pain treatment, new and different indications for legitimate medical use, the increase in the average age of the citizenry, new delivery methods and formulations for opioid pain relievers, new product development, and exportation. Thus, decreased production is not viewed as a realistic means to reduce diversion.

[20] Nonmedical use involves obtaining the drugs without a legitimate prescription and taking them while not under medical supervision.

[21] Prescription opioid death data for 2006 are the most current estimates.

[22] The 2006 data include more than 1,000 overdose deaths attributed to heroin and clandestinely produced fentanyl that was distributed in some Midwest, Great Lakes, and Mid-Atlantic cities.

[23] DEA investigations indicate that dubious pain clinics haveuniquecharacteristics,some of which includethe ability to quickly relocate, vague ormisleading ownership records,form nearly exclusive association with specific pharmacies, use specific physicians, cash-based payment methods, and rapid examinations.

[24] The $17.2 billion estimate is based on a review of U.S. banknotes repatriated from Mexico. The estimate represents only U.S. currency returned to the United States, not all U.S. currency that was smuggled to or through Mexico. This estimate is based on analysis of U.S. banknotes purchased by U.S. financial institutions from Mexican financial institutions from 2003 through 2004.

[25] SWIFT—Society for Worldwide Interbank Financial Telecommunication—is one of several payment messaging systems operating in the United States. SWIFT provides a secure communications platform for banks but does not actually hold or transfer funds.

[26] The cover payment method divides the message into two parts. Detailed funds-transfer instructions are sent directly to the beneficiary's bank via a SWIFT MT 103, while a second message, the SWIFT 202, is sent through all intermediary banks.

[27] Using serial payments, one financial institution transmits the funds-transfer instructions via a SWIFT MT 103 message to the intermediary bank. Each institution involved in this process receives the same level of detail about the transaction at each step.

[28] Intermediary banks, also called correspondent banks, allow banks to do business with each other if they do not have a direct relationship.

[29] In the past, other virtual worlds have included "virtual banks," but these functioned only as an element of the game and were not part of the real-world financial system. Prior to the issuance of this banking license, players of this virtual world could exchange real money for the virtual currency used in the game. Players could also earn money in the game by buying and selling objects or completing tasks such as hunting and mining. Earned virtual currency could be cashed out of the game at a fixed exchange rate to the U.S. dollar.

[30] Currently, 40 states either have operating PDMPs or have passed legislation to implement them.

In: National Drug Threat Assessment ...   ISBN: 978-1-60876-065-7
Editor: Paul Ziegler   © 2011 Nova Science Publishers, Inc.

Chapter 2

INTERNATIONAL DRUG CONTROL POLICY

Liana Sun Wyler

SUMMARY

The global illegal drug trade represents a multi-dimensional challenge that has implications for U.S. national interests as well as the international community. Common illegal drugs trafficked internationally include cocaine, heroin, and methamphetamine. According to the U.S. intelligence community, international drug trafficking can undermine political and regional stability and bolster the role and capabilities of organized crime in the drug trade. Key regions of concern include Latin America and Afghanistan, which are focal points in U.S. efforts to combat the production and transit of cocaine and heroin, respectively. Drug use and addiction have the potential to negatively affect the social fabric of communities, hinder economic development, and place an additional burden on national public health infrastructures.

As an issue of international policy concern for more than a century, and as a subject of longstanding U.S. and multilateral policy commitment, U.S. counterdrug efforts have expanded to include a broad array of tools to attack the international drug trade. Such approaches include (1) combating the production of drugs at the source, (2) combating the flow of drugs in transit, (3) dismantling international illicit drug networks, and (4) creating incentives for international cooperation on drug control.

Congress is involved in all aspects of U.S. international drug control policy, regularly appropriating funds for counterdrug initiatives, conducting oversight activities on federal counterdrug programs, and legislating changes to agency authorities and other counterdrug policies. For FY2012, the Administration has requested from Congress approximately $26.2 billion for all federal drug control programs, of which $2.1 billion is requested for international programs, including civilian and military U.S. foreign assistance. An additional $3.9 billion is requested for interdiction programs related to intercepting and disrupting foreign drug shipments en route to the United States.

Through its appropriations and federal oversight responsibilities, the 112th Congress may chose to continue tackling several ongoing policy issues concerning U.S. international drug control policy, including

- the role of the Department of Defense in counterdrug foreign assistance;
- challenges associated with sequencing alternative development and eradication programs;
- the effectiveness of U.S. efforts to promote international drug control cooperation; and
- how to reduce drug trafficking-related violence and other harmful manifestations of the drug trade.

The 112th Congress may also choose to address authorizing legislation for the White House's Office of National Drug Control Policy (ONDCP), which, pursuant to Section 714 of P.L. 105-277, as amended, expired at the end of FY2010. ONDCP's primary purpose is to establish policies, priorities, and objectives for the overall U.S. drug control program, including domestic and international aspects.

GLOBAL SCOPE OF THE PROBLEM

Illegal drugs refer to narcotic, psychotropic, and related substances whose production, sale, and use are restricted by domestic law and international drug control agreements.[1] Common illegal drugs trafficked internationally include cocaine, heroin, and synthetic drugs. International trade in these drugs represents a lucrative and what at times seems to be an intractable criminal enterprise.

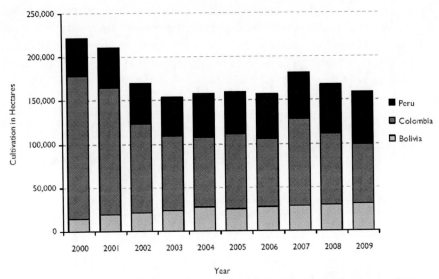

Source: U.N. Office on Drugs and Crime (UNODC), *World Drug Report* (2010), p.
162.

Notes: Coca bush is the harvestable crop used in the production of cocaine, crack
cocaine, and coca paste. **Figure 1** presents U.N.-published data on estimated illicit
coca bush available internationally for harvest after eradication. UNODC draws
on several sources of data for these estimates, and changes in data collection
methodologies may make estimates incomparable over time. For Bolivia, sources
through 2002 included the Inter-American Drug Abuse Control Commission and
the U.S. government. Since 2002 for the Yungas region and for all regions of
Bolivia since 2003 estimates were conducted by the National Illicit Crop
Monitoring System, supported by the UNODC. For Colombia and Peru, estimates
were conducted by the National Illicit Crop Monitoring System, supported by the
UNODC. The U.S. government publishes separate estimates of illicit coca bush
cultivation. See **Appendix A** for a comparison of U.N. versus U.S. estimates.

Figure 1. U.N. Estimates of Coca Bush Cultivation, 2000-2009.

Drug Cultivation and Production Trends

Both cocaine and heroin are plant-derived drugs, cultivated and harvested
by farmers in typically low-income countries or in regions of the world with
uneven economic development and a history of conflict. Coca bush, the plant
from which cocaine is derived, is mainly cultivated in three South American
countries: Colombia, Peru, and Bolivia. See **Figure 1** (see also **Appendix A**

for a comparison of U.N. and U.S. drug cultivation and production data).
During the past decade, Colombia has been the primary source of coca bush
cultivation. According to the United Nations, however, Colombia's proportion
of the world's total illegal coca bush cultivation has declined from
approximately 74% in 2000 to 43% in 2009.

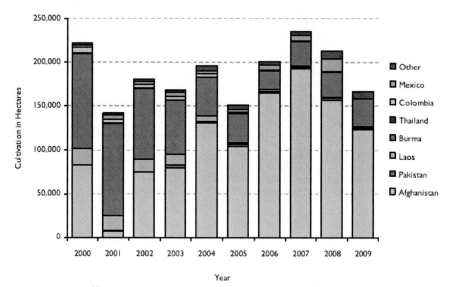

Source: U.N. Office on Drugs and Crime (UNODC), *World Drug Report* (2010), p.
    138.
Notes: Opium poppy is the harvestable crop used in the production of opiates,
    including opium and heroin. Figure 2 presents U.N.-published data on estimated
    illicit opium poppy available internationally for harvest after eradication. UNODC
    draws on several sources of data for these estimates, and changes in data
    collection methodologies may make estimates incomparable over time. For full
    sourcing details, see UNODC's 2010 *World Drug Report*. Note that 2009
    estimates do not include totals for Mexico. Countries and regions included in the
    "Other" category are Algeria, the Baltic countries, the Balkans, Central Asia and
    the Caucasus, Egypt, Guatemala, Iraq, Lebanon, Peru, Russia and member states
    of the Commonwealth of Independent States, South Asia, Thailand (beginning in
    2003), Ukraine, Venezuela, and Vietnam. The U.S. government publishes separate
    estimates of illicit opium poppy cultivation. See **Appendix A** for a comparison of
    U.N. versus U.S. estimates.

Figure 2. U.N. Estimates of Opium Poppy Cultivation, 2000-2009.

Table 1. Regional Drug Consumption: Opiates, Cocaine, and Synthetics Estimated Number of People, Aged 15-64, who Used Opiates or Cocaine at Least Once in 2008.

Region	Opiates		Cocaine		Synthetics	
	low estimate	high estimate	low estimate	high estimate	low estimate	high estimate
Africa	680,000	2,930,000	1,020,000	2,670,000	1,550,000	5,200,000
Asia	6,460,000	12,540,000	430,000	2,270,000	4,430,000	37,990,000
Europe	3,290,000	3,820,000	4,570,000	4,970,000	2,500,000	3,190,000
Latin America	1,000,000	1,070,000	2,560,000	2,910,000	1,670,000	2,690,000
North America	1,290,000	1,380,000	6,170,000	6,170,000	3,090,000	3,200,000
Oceania	120,000	150,000	330,000	390,000	470,000	630,000
Global	**12,840,000**	**21,880,000**	**15,070,000**	**19,380,000**	**13,710,000**	**52,900,000**

Source: U.N. Office on Drugs and Crime (UNODC), *World Drug Report* (2010), pp. 153, 173, and 214.

Notes: Global prevalence of opiate use, as a percentage of population totals, is between 0.3% and 0.5% (lower and upper ranges). Subregions where prevalence is potentially higher than average include Eastern Africa (1.3% at the upper range), the Near and Middle East (1.5% at the upper range), and Eastern/South-East Europe (0.9% at the upper range). Global prevalence of cocaine use, as a percentage of population totals, is between 0.3% and 0.4% (lower and upper ranges). Subregions where prevalence is potentially higher than average include North America (2.0% at the upper range), Oceania (1.7% at the upper range), Western/Central Europe (1.5% at the upper range), the Caribbean (1.2% at the upper range), and South America (1.0% at the upper range). Global prevalence of synthetics (amphetamine-, methamphetamine-, and ecstasy-group substances) use, as a percentage of population totals, is between 0.3% and 1.2% (lower and upper ranges). Subregions where prevalence is potentially higher than average include Oceania (2.8% at the upper range), the Caribbean (1.9% at the upper range), and East/Southeast Asia (1.4% at the upper range).

Estimates of harvestable coca bush are used to calculate how much 100% pure cocaine could theoretically be produced each year, based on the potency of sampled coca leaves and the efficiency of clandestine labs, where the plant is chemically processed into cocaine. According to United Nations estimates, the global total potential manufacture of pure cocaine in 2009 ranged between 842 to 1,111 metric tons, with Colombia alone manufacturing some 410 metric tons.[2] This represents roughly a stable trend in total potential manufacture of cocaine, compared to 2008 estimates.

Opium poppy, the plant from which opiates including heroin are derived, is cultivated mainly in Southwest Asia (Afghanistan and Pakistan) and Southeast Asia (Burma/Myanmar and Laos). (See Figure 2.) Opium poppy is also cultivated in Mexico, Guatemala, and Colombia, almost exclusively for heroin consumption in the United States. Over the past decade, Afghanistan has risen to prominence as the primary global source of illicit opium poppy cultivation, supplanting Burma, where the majority of opium poppy cultivation took place in the 1990s. In 2009, Afghanistan cultivated approximately 74% of the world's total illegal opium poppy. Similar to estimates to calculate potential cocaine manufacture, estimates are also used to calculate potential opium and potential heroin manufacture. According to the United Nations, the global total potential manufacture of opium in 2009 is estimated at 7,754 metric tons and the total potential manufacture of heroin (of unknown purity) in 2009 is estimated at 634 metric tons.[3]

Global illegal synthetic drug production is difficult to estimate. In general, the underlying chemicals needed for the production of synthetic drugs such as amphetamine, methamphetamine, and ecstasy[4] are legally manufactured in industrial factories for legitimate commercial and pharmaceutical purposes. In turn, some portion of the total legal production of these chemicals is diverted and misused for illicit purposes. Such diverted chemicals typically are processed into illegal synthetic drugs in clandestine laboratories, which can range in size from small residential-sized kitchens to large-scale "superlabs" capable of processing high volumes of synthetic drugs. According to the United Nations, however, the "variety and easy accessibility of the starting materials needed to manufacture synthetic drugs allow production to occur virtually anywhere in the world."[5]

Drug Trafficking and Consumption Trends

Major trafficking routes connect the drug producers with the drug consumers, with often sophisticated drug trafficking organizations (DTOs) controlling the various aspects of the supply chain. Current major drug transit pathways flow through Mexico and Central America (for drugs produced in South America and destined for the United States), West Africa (for South American cocaine destined for Europe and Afghan heroin en route to Europe and the United States), and all the countries surrounding Afghanistan (heroin destined to Europe, Eurasia, and elsewhere).

Globally, between 155 and 250 million people, aged 15 to 64, used illicit substances, including cannabis, at least once in 2008.[6] North America has traditionally been the main consumer of cocaine and cocaine-type drugs, with Europe's demand for cocaine rising in recent years. Europe and Asia have been the traditional markets for opiate-type drugs, including heroin. Asia and North America have been major markets for synthetic drugs. See Table 1 for regional breakdowns. Among these users, approximately 16 to 38 million are termed "problem drug users."[7] The latter category of individuals are responsible for the consumption of most illegal drugs. The majority of these problem drug users (an estimated 11 to 34 million) do not receive treatment.

Consequences of the Drug Trade

The global illegal drug trade represents a multi-dimensional challenge that has implications for U.S. national interests as well as the international community. Drug use and addiction have been said to negatively affect the social fabric of communities, hinder economic development, and place an additional burden on national public health infrastructures. According to the United Nations, drugs are both a cause and consequence of poverty, with "22 of the 34 countries least likely to achieve the Millennium Development Goals ... located in regions that are magnets for drug cultivation and trafficking."[8] Intravenous drug users are at particular risk of contracting diseases such as Hepatitis B, Hepatitis C, and HIV/AIDS. According to a recent study, as much as 31% of injecting drug users may be living with HIV, representing as much as 18% of the total number of people internationally living with HIV.[9]

Observers suggest that drug trafficking also represents a systemic threat to international security. Revenue from the illegal drug trade provides international DTOs with the resources to evade government detection;

undermine and co-opt legitimate social, political, and economic systems through corruption, extortion, or more violent forms of influence; penetrate legitimate economic structures through money laundering; and, in some instances, challenge the authority of national governments. In the process, a transnational network of criminal safe havens are established in which DTOs operate with impunity. As in the recent emergence of West Africa as a major cocaine transit hub for Latin American drug traffickers, DTOs prey on states with low capacity for effective governance or the enforcement of the rule of law. This can exacerbate preexisting political instability, post-conflict environments, and economic vulnerability.

DRUG TRAFFICKING ORGANIZATIONS (DTOs)

The U.S. National Drug Threat Assessment defines DTOs as "complex organizations with highly defined command-and-control structures that produce, transport, and/or distribute large quantities of one or more illicit drugs." [10]

In addition to moving illicit drugs, DTOs are capable of generating, moving, and laundering billions of dollars in drug proceeds annually. Major DTOs of concern to the United States include Mexican and Colombian DTOs, which are responsible for the production and transport of most illicit drugs into the United States. Other major DTOs of concern include the West African/Nigerian DTOs and Southwest and East Asian DTOs.

While DTOs are commonly identified by their nationality of origin, they are known to be aggressively transnational and poly-criminal— seeking to expand their consumer markets, to diversify their criminal enterprises and product variety, and to explore new transit points and safe havens with low law enforcement capacity and high corruption. Many of them also have links to other illicit actors, including arms traffickers, money launderers, terrorists and insurgent groups, and corrupt officials.

By many accounts, drug trafficking, state weakness, political corruption, and powerful DTOs are part of a seemingly self-perpetuating cycle. [11] On the one hand, a drug trafficking presence in a country can increase corruption and undermine political stability, while on the other hand, social and political instability may be causal factors for attracting a thriving drug industry. Further, academic literature on conflict duration indicates that control of a lucrative illegal drug trade in the hands of a particular political actor, rebel, or insurgent group can lengthen a conflict. State powers in the hands of a DTO through deeply entrenched kleptocracy serve as a force multiplier to enhance a DTO's power by harnessing the capacity of a state's infrastructure—roads, seaports, airports, warehouses, security apparatus, justice sector, and international political sovereignty—to further the DTO's illicit business aims.

The consequences of a thriving illicit drug trade co-located in a U.S. combat zone are illustrated today in Afghanistan, where some portion of drug-related proceeds annually help facilitate the current insurgency.[12] In other regions, such as in the Western Hemisphere, Americans have been murdered, taken hostage, and tortured for their involvement in counternarcotics operations—highlighting the past and ongoing dangers associated with the international drug trade.[13] In addition, many observers are concerned about the potential spread of DTO-related violence from Mexico into the United States.[14] Moreover, several groups listed by the U.S. Department of State as Foreign Terrorist Organizations (FTOs) are known to be involved in drug trafficking.

2011 U.S. INTELLIGENCE ASSESSMENT OF THE DRUG THREAT

James R. Clapper, the Director of National Intelligence, presented the intelligence community's annual threat assessment to Congress in February 2011 and highlighted, among other issues, narco-threats to political and regional stability, illicit finance for insurgents and terrorist groups, and the expanding role and capabilities of organized crime in the illicit drug trade.[15] The threat assessment made reference to the following key trends:

- The drug threat to the United States, principally driven by "strong U.S. demand for illicit drugs," stems mainly from the Western Hemisphere: Mexico, Colombia, Canada, and the United States.
- Despite significant successes against Mexican drug cartels, "Mexico's overall military and police capabilities remain inadequate to break the trafficking organizations and contain criminal violence."
- Efforts to discourage Afghan farmers from cultivating opium poppy will have limited effect due high opium prices, the inability to implement alternative livelihood programs on a large scale due to

insecurity, and the absence of a market infrastructure in key poppy-growing regions.

- Drug trafficking is a major problem in Africa, as traffickers continue to use West Africa as a transit point for Latin American cocaine destined for Europe. Systematic, high-level cooptation of government and law enforcement officials facilitates the African drug trade, with Guinea-Bissau identified as "Africa's first narco-state."

- Terrorists and insurgents are predicted to "increasingly" turn to crime to generate funds and acquire logistical support. Examples of such groups, which are dependent on drug trafficking proceeds to remain viable as terrorist and insurgent organizations, include the Taliban and the Revolutionary Armed Forces of Colombia (FARC).

STRATEGIC GUIDANCE

Drug trafficking has been an issue of international policy concern for more than a century and a subject of longstanding U.S. and multilateral policy commitment. Yet, tensions continue to appear at times between U.S. foreign drug policy and approaches advocated by independent observers and the international community.

Many U.S. policymakers have argued that the confluence of political and security threats surrounding international drug trafficking necessitates a policy posture that emphasizes the disruption and dismantlement of the criminal actors and organizations involved in all aspects of the drug trade. At the same time, other observers and policymakers have argued that security and law enforcement approaches to international drug control have failed to achieve notable successes in "eliminating or reducing significantly" the supply of illicit drugs—a goal the United Nations committed in 1998 to achieve by 2008 (and in 2009, recommitted to achieve by 2019).[16]

The United Nations Office on Drugs and Crime (UNODC), for example, argues that international concern with "public security" during the past decade has overshadowed other key tenets of drug control policy, including public health and drug demand reduction.[17] Numerous international non-governmental organizations (NGOs) also argue that greater emphasis should be placed on policies that emphasize efforts to reduce health and social consequences; programs to promote treatment, rehabilitation, and social re-integration for drug users; as well as sustainable and comprehensive alternative development projects.[18]

Some advocates are calling for a reevaluation of current international drug policies.[19] Such calls for a new look at international drug policies are being advocated from an increasingly growing sector of the policy community.[20] It remains unclear whether such policy debates can translate into lasting improvements to reduce the production, trafficking, use, and consequences of illegal drug trade. However, changes could affect a range of foreign policy considerations for the United States, including foreign aid reform, counterinsurgency strategy (particularly in Afghanistan), the distribution of domestic and international drug control funding, and the relative balance of civilian, law enforcement, and military roles in anti-drug efforts.

International Policy Framework

Efforts to combat drug trafficking have enjoyed a longstanding and robust commitment internationally. One of the first multilateral efforts to combat drugs began with the International Opium Commission of 1909. Since then, the international community has broadened and deepened the scope of international drug control through several international treaties and monitoring mechanisms.

Today, international drug control efforts are grounded on the policy foundations laid by three United Nations treaties: the 1961 Single Convention on Narcotic Drugs, as amended; the 1971 Convention on Psychotropic Substances; and the 1988 Convention Against Illicit Traffic in Narcotic Drugs and Psychotropic Substances. More than 95% of U.N. member states, including the United States, are parties to these three international drug control treaties.[21]

In combination, these U.N. treaties limit the international production and trade of a defined set of narcotic drugs, psychotropic substances, and the precursor chemicals used to make these substances for primarily medical and scientific purposes. The treaties also establish international mechanisms to monitor treaty adherence—through the International Narcotics Control Board (INCB)—and for the collection of data related to the illicit cultivation, production, and manufacture of proscribed drugs.

U.N. policymaking on drug-related matters take place through the U.N. Commission on Narcotic Drugs, which is a functional commission of the U.N. Economic and Social Council. The U.N. Commission on Narcotic Drugs monitors global drug trends, develops strategies for international drug control, and recommends measures to combat the world drug problem. To support

U.N. Member States in combating drugs, the UNODC conducts field-based technical assistance projects internationally and conducts research and analysis on current drug market trends.

KEY U.N. TREATIES AND ENTITIES FOR INTERNATIONAL DRUG CONTROL

- 1961 Single Convention on Narcotic Drugs, as amended
- 1971 Convention on Psychotropic Substances
- 1988 Convention Against Illicit Traffic in Narcotic Drugs and Psychotropic Substances
- International Narcotics Control Board
- U.N. Commission on Narcotic Drugs
- U.N. Office on Drugs and Crime

Regional counterdrug-related organizations also supplement multilateral efforts globally. Such efforts include the Inter-American Drug Abuse Control Commission (CICAD), which is the drug control arm of the Organization of American States (OAS), and the Drug Advisory Programme (DAP) of the Colombo Plan. CICAD serves as the regional policy forum for all aspects of Western Hemisphere illegal drug issues. DAP supports drug demand reduction, treatment, and rehabilitation in the Asia and Pacific regions. Related international efforts also reinforce counternarcotics policies through their cross-cutting focus on such transnational phenomena as money laundering, corruption, organized crime, and global health.

U.S. Foreign Policy Framework

The United States has been involved in international drug control since at least the beginning of the 20th century. Contemporary U.S. counternarcotics efforts were brought to the forefront of U.S. policy debates in the late 1960s. In 1971, President Richard Nixon declared that illicit drugs were America's "public enemy number one."[22] President Ronald Reagan followed with a directive in 1986 that identified narcotics trafficking a threat to U.S. national security.[23] Successive administrations have continued to feature combating the international drug trade prominently among U.S. foreign policy priorities. See

Appendix B for a discussion of specific U.S. agency roles in combating drugs internationally.

Since at least the late 1960s, Congress has also been active on drug policy issues, enacting key provisions in U.S. law that define U.S. policies and authorities relating to international narcotics control, exercising oversight responsibilities on U.S. counternarcotics policy, and appropriating funds for international counternarcotics programs.

In 1998, Congress established the Office of National Drug Control Policy (ONDCP) to coordinate all U.S. counterdrug policy, both domestically and internationally.[24] ONDCP's Director is the primary advisor to the President on drug policy issues. The State Department is statutorily designated as the lead U.S. agency responsible for international counterdrug foreign assistance, and the Defense Department is the lead in the detection and monitoring of foreign drug flows destined for the United States. The U.S. Drug Enforcement Administration (DEA) is the lead on drug-related law enforcement. Multiple other U.S. agencies are also responsible for various aspects of the U.S. counterdrug response.

The following sections describe several of the key U.S. government strategies and initiatives for combating drugs internationally and in specific key regions around the world.

U.S. National Drug Control Strategy

U.S. involvement in international drug control rests on the central premise that helping foreign governments combat the illegal drug trade abroad will ultimately curb illegal drug availability and use in the United States. To this end, the current Administration maintains the goal of reducing and eliminating the international flow of illegal drugs into the United States through international cooperation to disrupt the drug trade and interdiction efforts.

Since 1999, Congress has required that the White House, through the Office of National Drug Control Policy (ONDCP), submit to Congress a National Drug Control Strategy report each year.[25] This strategy describes the total budget for drug control programs—both domestically and internationally—and outlines U.S. strategic goals for stemming drug supply and demand.

The international component of the Administration's 2010 National Drug Control Strategy centers on three specific "principles," or goals: (1) collaborate with international partners to disrupt the drug trade, (2) support drug control efforts of major drug source and transit countries, and (3) attack key vulnerabilities of drug trafficking organizations (DTOs). The 2010

National Drug Control Strategy is also particularly notable for its admission that the United States, due to U.S. domestic consumption of illegal drugs, bears responsibility, in conjunction with drug-producing and -transit countries, for the existence of the international drug trade.[26]

2010 U.S. STRATEGIC "PRINCIPLES" AND "ACTIONS" TO COMBAT DRUGS INTERNATIONALLY

The 2010 National Drug Control Strategy lists three strategic principles and corollary actions to be achieved in reducing the international drug supply. They include the following:

Principle #1: Collaborate with International Partners to Disrupt the Drug Trade

Action A: Conduct Joint Counterdrug Operations
Action B: Strengthen Counterdrug Institutions in the Western Hemisphere
Action C: Disrupt Drug Flows in the Trans-Atlantic and Trans-Pacific Regions
Action D: Prevent Synthetic Drug Production and Precursor Chemical Diversion
Action E: Expand Prevention and Treatment Initiatives Bilaterally, Regionally, and Multilaterally
Action F: Expand Health Interventions for Injection Drug Users Internationally

Principle #2: Support the Drug Control Efforts of Major Drug Source and Transit Countries

Action A: Strengthen Strategic Partnerships with Mexico
Action B: Disrupt the Nexus Between Drugs, Insurgency, and Corruption in Afghanistan
Action C: Build Law Enforcement and Criminal Justice Capacities in Source Countries in the Americas
Action D: Implement the Caribbean Basin Security Initiative
Action E: Promote Alternative Livelihoods for Coca and Opium Farmers

Action F: Support the Central American Regional Security Initiative
Action G: Develop a Comprehensive Counterdrug Strategy for the Western Hemisphere
Action H: Consolidate Gains Made in Colombia

Principle #3: Attack Key Vulnerabilities of Drug Trafficking Organizations (DTOs)

Action A: Improve Intelligence on the Vulnerabilities of DTOs
Action B: Disrupt Illicit Drug Trafficking in the Transit Zone
Action C: Target the Illicit Finances of DTOs
Action D: Target Cartel Leadership

International Drug Control Strategy Report

As required by the Foreign Assistance Act of 1961, as amended, the State Department annually submits to Congress an International Drug Control Strategy Report (INCSR).[27] The INCSR, released in two volumes each year, provides an overview of U.S. counternarcotics policies and programs internationally. It also provides a country-by-country analysis of progress that foreign governments, particularly those of major drug-producing and drug-transit countries, have made in adhering to its international commitments to combat drugs (volume I) and related financial crimes (volume II).

The 2011 INCSR, released on March 3, 2011, reports that drug trafficking and transnational organized crime continue to threaten U.S. and citizen security interests, particularly as the profits that the drug trade generates remain the most lucrative criminal activity internationally. The INCSR also reports that while progress has been achieved in certain parts of the world, continued progress to combat drugs internationally requires ongoing cooperation and willingness to adapt to emerging threats.

Reported regional challenges to international drug control include combating drug trafficking in the Western Hemisphere, not only in historically established major drug source and transit countries such as Colombia and Mexico, but also in parts of Central America and the Caribbean, which have become vulnerable to exploitation as drug traffickers adapt and adjust to new smuggling corridors in the face of heightened enforcement pressure along old smuggling routes. The cultivation of opium poppy for heroin in Afghanistan also remains a global drug problem, despite improvements in the number of poppy-free provinces in Afghanistan in recent years.[28] Nevertheless, the INCSR reports that "active insurgences tied to drug traffickers in the southern and western provinces of Afghanistan overlap with 98 percent of the country's poppy cultivation."[29]

Other reported challenges to international drug control include dealing with new and emerging criminal activities and technologies designed to avoid detection. Such activities include the use of the Internet to facilitate drug trafficking, use of new precursors and chemicals in the production of illegal drugs, the development of self-propelled semi-submersible vessels designed specifically for smuggling drugs, and screening containers for illegal cargo.

Regional Initiatives

The majority of U.S. counterdrug efforts internationally are concentrated in two regions: South America and Afghanistan, which are focal points in U.S. efforts to combat the production and transit of cocaine and heroin, respectively. The U.S. government is also involved in developing several new counternarcotics programs, including in West Africa, the Caribbean (Caribbean Basin Security Initiative), and Central America (Central America Regional Security Initiative).

Plan Colombia, the Andean Counterdrug Program, and Ongoing Assistance

Plan Colombia was developed by the government of Colombia in 1999 as a six-year plan, concluding in 2005, to end the country's decades-long armed conflict, eliminate drug trafficking, and promote economic and social development. The plan aimed to curb trafficking activity and reduce coca cultivation in Colombia by 50% over five years.[30] Congress approved legislation in support of Plan Colombia in 2000, appropriating foreign assistance funds under the Andean Counterdrug Initiative (ACI) account each year ever since.[31] ACI historically provided counternarcotics assistance for Colombia, but also for other countries in the Andean region, including at various times Bolivia, Brazil, Ecuador, Panama, Peru, and Venezuela.[32] Beginning in FY2008, Congress renamed ACI the Andean Counterdrug Program (ACP) and then subsequently incorporated ACP into the International Narcotics Control and Law Enforcement (INCLE) foreign aid account. Since ACI and ACP were first implemented, U.S. counterdrug assistance has focused mainly on four strategic pillars:

1. eradicate coca and opium poppy crops,
2. interdict illegal drugs,

3. provide coca and opium poppy farmers other sources of income through alternative development, and

4. build institutions to train security forces and to strengthen democratic governance capacity.

For FY2012, ONDCP reports that the Administration is requesting $132.8 million for drug control assistance to Colombia.[33] Projects in FY2012 are intended to continue to support Colombia's National Consolidation Plan, the U.S.-Colombia Strategic Development Initiative, and the nationalization of previous U.S.-supported Colombian military programs, including the counterdrug brigade, Colombian Army aviation, and the air bridge denial program.

The Mérida Initiative and Beyond

The United States and Mexico announced on October 22, 2007, the start of a multiyear, bilateral security agreement called the Mérida Initiative.[34] This initiative aims to combat drug trafficking and other criminal activity along the U.S.-Mexican border, as well as in Central America.[35] Initial U.S. bilateral assistance to Mexico and Central America under the initiative consisted of a $1.4 billion, three-year security package ending in FY2010 that would provide two main forms of assistance: (1) equipment, including helicopters and surveillance aircraft, and technical resources to combat drug trafficking, and (2) training and technical advice for Mexican and Central American military, judicial, and law enforcement officials.[36]

In mid-January 2010, the State Department approved a new strategy for Mexico as a follow-on to the Mérida Initiative after it ended in FY2010, called Beyond Mérida.[37] Follow-on counterdrug support to Central America would be provided through a separate program called the Central American Regional Security Initiative (CARSI). For the follow-on assistance program to Mexico, the character of U.S. support shifted from a focus on major counternarcotics equipment acquisition that was designed to improve operational ability against drug traffickers to a longer-term emphasis on institutional development and capacity building to the Mexican justice sector. This shift included greater emphasis on social reforms that can galvanize community support to fight organized crime, including drug trafficking.[38] The Beyond Mérida strategy has four pillars:

1. disrupt and dismantle organized criminal groups;
2. institutionalize justice sector reforms to sustain the rule of law and respect for human rights;
3. create an efficient, economically competitive border crossing that ensures "secure two-way flows" of travelers and trade; and
4. support Mexican government efforts to build strong and resilient communities through community organizations, civil society participation, sustainable economic opportunities, community cohesion, and violence reduction.

For FY2012, ONDCP reports that the Administration is requesting $66 million for drug control assistance to Mexico.[39] Programs are intended to support short-term goals of dismantling drug trafficking and other criminal organizations and the long-term goal of strengthening Mexico's justice sector institutions.

THE 2009 U.S. NATIONAL SOUTHWEST BORDER COUNTERNARCOTICS STRATEGY

In 2007, the U.S. government released an National Southwest Border Counternarcotics Strategy. This strategy outlined U.S. federal government roles and goals for preventing the illegal trafficking of drugs across the U.S.-Mexico border. ONDCP released an updated version of the Southwest Border Strategy in 2009, which took into account developments in bilateral U.S.-Mexico cooperation on drugs, particularly through the Mérida Initiative. In particular, the 2009 update expanded the U.S. counterdrug mission along the Southwest border to include not only combating the inbound flow of illegal drugs from Mexico into the United States, but also the outbound flow of illegal bulk cash and weapons destined for Mexico-based drug trafficking organizations. In order to achieve the strategic goal of substantially reducing the "flow of illicit drugs, drug proceeds, and associated instruments of violence across the Southwest border" the 2009 Strategy identifies six key objectives:

1. enhance intelligence capabilities associated with the Southwest border;
2. interdict drugs, drug proceeds, and related weapons at and between ports of entry, and in air and maritime domains along the Southwest border;

3. ensure the prosecution of all significant drug trafficking, money laundering, bulk currency, and weapons smuggling and trafficking cases;
4. disrupt and dismantle drug trafficking organizations;
5. enhance counterdrug technologies for drug detection and interdiction along the Southwest border; and
6. enhance U.S.-Mexico cooperation regarding joint counterdrug efforts.

Caribbean Basin Security Initiative

President Barack Obama announced the Caribbean Basin Security Initiative (CBSI) at the Summit of the Americas in April 2009 as a security cooperation effort in the Caribbean Basin region, focused on combating drug trafficking organizations, gangs, and other criminal groups.

Congress appropriated $37 million for the CBSI in FY2010 to variously combat drug trafficking and organized crime, strengthen the rule of law, and promote social justice. The Obama Administration's FY2011 request for CBSI is $79 million, of which $31.2 million was requested for the State Department to conduct the counterdrug aspects of CBSI. For FY2012, ONDCP reports that the Administration is requesting $17.8 million for drug control assistance through the CBSI.[40] Drug control funding reportedly would support regional counternarcotics initiatives, including efforts to improve regional capacity to interdict and eradicate drugs, reduce local demand for drugs, as well as to counter money laundering and corruption.[41]

Central American Regional Security Initiative

The Central America Regional Security Initiative (CARSI) is a follow-on to anti-crime assistance provided to the region originally through the Mérida Initiative. CARSI, through bilateral and regional efforts, seeks support efforts designed to stop corrosive and interrelated effects of crime, drugs, violence, and corruption the region. According to the State Department's 2010 International Narcotics Control Strategy Report, CARSI will extend U.S. commitments to assistance Central American states to combat criminal organizations, gangs, and related-violence in the region; to support justice sector capacity building; and to improve law enforcement intelligence sharing within and among regional governments.[42] The stated five goals of CARSI are to

1. create safe streets and emphasize citizen safety;
2. disrupt the movement of criminals and contraband throughout Central America;
3. support the institutional capacity of governments in the region;
4. reestablish effective state presence and security in communities at risk; and
5. foster enhanced levels of coordination and cooperation among countries in Central America for security and rule of law efforts.[43]

Table 2. Federal Drug Control Funding, FY2010 Final-FY2012 Request budget authority in $U.S. millions.

Activities	FY2010 Final	FY2011 Est.	FY2012 Req.
International	2,595.0	2,367.5	2,138.4
Interdiction	3,658.0	3,706.7	3,901.0
Domestic	19,634.1	19,657.4	20,170.3
Total	25,887.1	25,731.6	26,209.7

Source: Adapted from Office of National Drug Control Policy (ONDCP), National Drug Control Budget, FY2012 Funding Highlights, February 2011. Totals may not add due to rounding.

Note: "International" activities refers to activities primarily focused on or conducted in areas outside the United States, mainly conducted by the State Department, U.S. Agency for International Development (USAID), Defense Department, and Department of Justice. International activities include a wide range of drug control programs to eradicate crops, seize drugs (except air and riverine interdiction seizures), arrest and prosecute major traffickers, destroy processing capabilities, develop and promote alternative crops to replace drug crops, reduce demand, investigate money laundering and financial crime activities, and promote the involvement of other nations in efforts to control the supply of and demand for drugs. "Interdiction" refers to activities designed to intercept and disrupt shipments of illegal drugs and their precursors en route to the United States from abroad. "Domestic" refers to activities related to domestic demand reduction, including federal drug treatment and drug prevention programs, as well as domestic law enforcement.

Of the total amount appropriated for CARSI, $12.1 million in FY2009 was appropriated for counternarcotics-specific purposes in the region. In FY2010, an estimated $27 million was appropriated. The Administration requested an additional $31 million for FY2011. For FY2011, the State Department requests funds for counternarcotics-specific purposes in order to continue support for U.S.-vetted units of local law enforcement officers in the region; demand reduction programs; existing aviation assets in Guatemala for monitoring drug flows; and enhanced regional land and maritime interdiction capabilities and logistics supports.[44]

Table 3. Federal Drug Control Funding, FY2005 Actual-FY2011 Request budget authority in $U.S. millions.

Activities	FY2005	FY2006	FY2007	FY2008	FY2009	FY2010 Enact.	FY2011 Req.
International	1,393.3	1,434.5	2,050.2	1,824.6	2,082.2	2,288.0	2,308.1
Interdiction	2,928.7	3,287.0	3,175.9	2,901.4	3,910.2	3,640.1	3,727.0
Domestic	8,462.2	8,422.6	8,618.0	8,550.3	9,286.0	9,103.4	9,517.5
Total	12,784.2	13,844.1	13,844.1	13,276.3	15,278.4	15,031.5	15,552.5

Source: Adapted from Office of National Drug Control Policy (ONDCP), National Drug Control Strategy, FY2011 Budget Summary, 2010. Totals may not add due to rounding.

Afghanistan Counterdrug Strategy

Drug control policy in Afghanistan has undergone a shift in strategy since June 2009, when the late Ambassador Richard Holbrooke, who at the time was the Obama Administration's Special Representative for Afghanistan and Pakistan, announced a halt to U.S. eradication efforts in Afghanistan and a concurrent increase in priority to agricultural development (or alternative livelihoods) assistance as well as interdiction.[45] The drug policy shift was formalized with the release of the Afghanistan and Pakistan Regional Stabilization Strategy in January 2010, which connects U.S. counternarcotics policy with U.S. counterinsurgency goals in the region. The January 2010 Regional Strategy had sections on combating the Afghan narcotics trade and disrupting illicit financial flows, among others.[46] The most significant changes in the January 2010 strategy include the elimination of U.S.-led eradication as a strategic goal, the addition as a key initiative of increasing U.S. government personnel in Afghanistan (particularly DEA), and the enhancement civilian-military coordination with new coordination centers in London, Kabul, and Kandahar. Key initiatives to disrupt illicit financial flows include the Illicit Finance Task Force[47] and the Afghanistan Threat Finance Cell.

In March 2010, the State Department released an updated U.S. Counternarcotics Strategy for Afghanistan. It outlined two strategic goals—(1) counter the narcotics-insurgency nexus and (2) counter the narcotics-corruption nexus—coupled with several related objectives. Reiterating the January 2010 Regional Strategy, the March 2010 Counternarcotics Strategy confirms the U.S. government's decision to "no longer fund or support large-

scale eradication of poppy fields," while condoning Afghan-led local
eradication.[48] The March 2010 Counternarcotics Strategy also emphasized the
need to improve the connection between the U.S. government's
counternarcotics goals with the U.S. government's counterinsurgency goals.
To this end, ONDCP reports that the Administration is requesting $102.6
million for FY2012 drug control assistance to Afghanistan.[49]

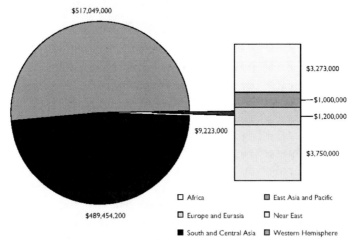

$517,049,000

$3,273,000

$1,000,000

$1,200,000

$9,223,000

$3,750,000

□ Africa   ▨ East Asia and Pacific

$489,454,200   □ Europe and Eurasia   □ Near East

■ South and Central Asia   ▨ Western Hemisphere

Source: U.S. Department of State, Office of the Director of Foreign Assistance (F),
    response to CRS request, March 2011.

Note: Data included in this chart represent all State Department FY2008, FY2009, and
    FY2010 Operational Plan updates as of March 15, 2011 (0100 EST). In FY2007,
    plans were completed by all USAID offices except Iraq and by some State
    Department offices. FY 2009 GHCS-State and GHCS-USAID account values do
    not currently include funds reported in the COPRS system for the PEPFAR
    program.

Figure 3. U.S. Civilian Counternarcotics Assistance, by Region, FY2010
Operational Plan Estimates for the State Department and USAID Only.

Counternarcotics Support to West Africa

While Africa has historically held a peripheral role in the transnational
illicit drug trade, drug traffickers have begun to view West Africa as a
strategically placed transit and staging point along cocaine trafficking routes
from South America to Europe.[50] While there is no region-wide initiative in
place to combat the growing drug trade through West Africa, the State
Department requested $13.2 million for counternarcotics assistance in Africa
in FY2011, up from about $0.5 million in FY2006. At the same time, the

Department of Defense (DOD) has reportedly allocated $21.1 million in FY2010 and $30 million in FY2011 to counternarcotics programs in Sub-Saharan Africa.

OVERALL U.S. DRUG CONTROL FUNDING

For FY2012, the Administration has requested approximately $26.2 billion for all federal drug control programs, up from $25.9 billion in FY2010 (see Table 2).[51] Of this, 23%, or $6 billion, is requested for international and interdiction programs. Beginning with the FY2012 budget request, ONDCP significantly restructured its budgeting process, adding 19 more agencies and programs to the overall drug budget.[52] According to ONDCP, these additional agencies had not previously been included in the drug budget because the programs were deemed to be "unreliably estimated or were thought to be related to consequences of drug use (as opposed to directly related to drug use reduction)."[53] The addition of these agencies had the effect of increasing the total budget, particularly domestic programs (compare Table 2 with Table 3).

U.S. ASSISTANCE FOR INTERNATIONAL COUNTERNARCOTICS PROGRAMS

A large component of the international component of ONDCP's national drug budget, discussed above, is committed to civilian- and military-funded assistance to foreign countries for counterdrug support. Such foreign aid is designed to support foreign countries interdict and eradicate drugs, support the development of alternative livelihoods, and reduce the local demand for drugs. The following sections describe both civilian and military funding and authorities for counternarcotics foreign assistance.

Civilian Funding and Authorities

The U.S. Department of State and U.S. Agency for International Development (USAID) are the two primary sources of civilian U.S. funding for international counternarcotics assistance. Counternarcotics programs may be implemented by other U.S. government entities or to private contractors.

Funding spigots include the foreign aid accounts for Development Assistance
(DA); Economic Support Fund (ESF); Assistance for Europe, Eurasia, and
Central Asia (AEECA); and International Narcotics Control and Law
Enforcement (INCLE).

**Table 4. U.S. Civilian Counternarcotics Assistance, by Region, FY2007-
FY2010 Operational Plan Estimates for the State Department and USAID
Only.**

	FY2007	FY2008	FY2009	FY2010
Sub-Saharan Africa	200,000	1,592,000	1,110,000	3,273,000
East Asia and Pacific	600,000	2,317,000	1,000,000	1,000,000
Europe and Eurasia	—	1,269,000	887,000	1,200,000
Near East	—	—	—	3,750,000
South and Central Asia	4,000,000	317,934,046	454,125,000	489,454,200
Western Hemisphere	527,429,000	540,843,000	401,343,100	517,049,000
TOTAL	532,229,000	863,955,046	858,465,100	1,015,726,200

Source: U.S. Department of State, Office of the Director of Foreign Assistance (F),
    response to CRS request, July 2010.
Note: Data included in this chart represent all State Department FY2008, FY2009, and
    FY2010 Operational Plan updates as of March 15, 2011 (0100 EST). In FY2007,
    plans were completed by all USAID offices except Iraq and by some State
    Department offices. FY 2009 GHCS-State and GHCS-USAID account values do
    not currently include funds reported in the COPRS system for the PEPFAR
    program.

Authority for the U.S. Department of State and USAID is derived from
multiple provisions in the Foreign Assistance Act (FAA) of 1961, as amended.
Key provisions are located at Chapter 8 of Part I of the FAA, as amended,
entitled "International Narcotics Control." Section 481 of the FAA states that
the Secretary of State is "responsible for coordinating all assistance provided
by the United States Government to support international efforts to combat
illicit narcotics production or trafficking." Section 126 of the FAA also directs
USAID, when planning programs of assistance for countries in which illicit
narcotics cultivation takes place, to "give priority consideration to programs

which would help reduce illicit narcotics cultivation by stimulating broader development opportunities."

Figure 3 and Figure 4 depict civilian assistance for international counternarcotics programs in FY2010 by region and by program. Table 4 and Table 5 summarizes trends in civilian assistance for international counternarcotics programs from FY2007 through FY2010.

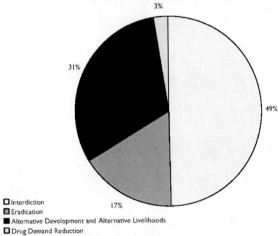

Source: U.S. Department of State, Office of the Director of Foreign Assistance (F), response to CRS request, March 2011.

Note: Data included in this chart represent all State Department FY2008, FY2009, and FY2010 Operational Plan updates as of March 15, 2011 (0100 EST). In FY2007, plans were completed by all USAID offices except Iraq and by some State Department offices. FY 2009 GHCS-State and GHCS-USAID account values do not currently include funds reported in the COPRS system for the PEPFAR program.

Figure 4. U.S. Civilian Counternarcotics Assistance, by Function, FY2010 Operational Plan Estimates for the State Department and USAID Only.

Military Funding and Authorities

The U.S. Department of Defense (DOD) has multiple roles and responsibilities in the area of counternarcotics. Pursuant to 10 U.S.C. 124, DOD is the single lead federal agency for the detection and monitoring of aerial and maritime movement of illegal drugs toward the United States and plays a key role in collecting, analyzing, and sharing intelligence on illegal drugs with U.S. law enforcement and international security counterparts. In addition, Congress authorizes DOD to offer counternarcotics assistance to train and equip foreign countries in their efforts to build institutional capacity and control ungoverned spaces used by drug traffickers.

**Table 5. U.S. Civilian Counternarcotics Assistance, by Function,
FY2007-FY2010 Operational Plan Estimates
for the State Department and USAID Only**

	FY2007	FY2008	FY2009	FY2010
Interdiction	165,181,000	185,853,880	225,364,000	505,045,000
Eradication	202,952,000	331,245,000	261,166,000	169,227,000
Alternative Development and Alternative Livelihoods	134,766,957	274,480,258	328,577,100	314,939,000
Drug Demand Reduction	3,734,000	15,766,000	43,358,000	26,515,200
Program Design and Learning	25,595,043	652,000	—	—
Administration and Oversight	—	55,957,908	—	—
TOTAL	532,229,000	863,955,046	858,465,100	1,015,726,200

Source: U.S. Department of State, Office of the Director of Foreign Assistance (F), response to CRS request, March 2011.

Note: Data included in this chart represent all State Department FY2008, FY2009, and FY2010 Operational Plan updates as of March 15, 2011 (0100 EST). In FY2007, plans were completed by all USAID offices except Iraq and by some State Department offices. FY 2009 GHCS-State and GHCS-USAID account values do not currently include funds reported in the COPRS system for the PEPFAR program.

DOD maintains two counternarcotics foreign assistance training and/or equipping authorities, originating from Section 1004 of the National Defense Authorization Act (NDAA) for Fiscal Year 1991 (P.L. 101-510) and Section 1033 of the NDAA for FY1998 (P.L. 105-85). Under Section 1004, Congress authorized DOD to provide counterdrug-related training and transport of law enforcement personnel to foreign law enforcement agencies worldwide, among other provisions. Section 1033 enables DOD to assist specific countries' counterdrug efforts by providing nonlethal protective and utility personnel equipment, including navigation equipment, secure and non-secure communications equipment, radar equipment, night vision systems, vehicles, aircraft, and boats.

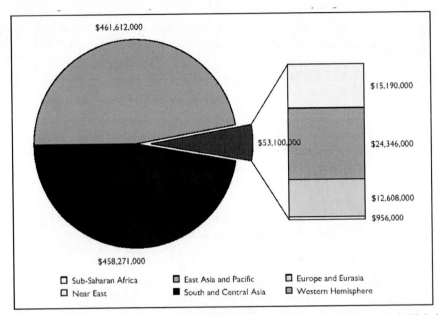

Source: U.S. Department of Defense (DOD), Office of Counternarcotics and Global Threats, response to CRS request, March 2011.
Note: This data reflect non-budget quality estimates of DOD counterdrug support provided or efforts in these countries/regions; DOD formal budget submissions to Congress do not measure counterdrug programs by countries/regions.

Figure 5. U.S. Military Counternarcotics Assistance, by Region, FY2010.

Currently, DOD is authorized to provide Section 1033 assistance to 22 countries, including (in chronological order) Peru and Colombia (Sec. 1033, P.L. 105-85); Afghanistan, Bolivia, Ecuador, Pakistan, Tajikistan, Turkmenistan, and Uzbekistan (Sec. 1021, P.L. 108-136); Azerbaijan, Kazakhstan, Kyrgyzstan, Armenia, Guatemala, Belize, and Panama (Sec. 1022, P.L. 109-364); Mexico and the Dominican Republic (Sec. 1022, P.L. 110-181); and Guinea Bissau, Senegal, El Salvador, and Honduras (Sec. 1024, P.L. 110-417).

Table 6. U.S. Military Counternarcotics Assistance, by Region, FY2007-FY2010.

	FY2007	FY2008	FY2009	FY2010
Sub-Saharan Africa	7,389,000	10,703,000	18,228,000	15,190,000
East Asia and Pacific	25,992,000	33,091,000	37,673,000	24,346,000
Europe and Eurasia	1,755,000	4,884,000	6,806,000	12,608,000
Near East	978,000	6,000	824,000	956,000
South and Central Asia	337,336,000	361,698,000	330,973,000	458,271,000
Western Hemisphere	394,903,000	405,624,000	484,330,000	461,612,000
TOTAL	768,353,000	816,006,000	878,834,000	972,983,000

Source: U.S. Department of Defense (DOD), Office of Counternarcotics and Global Threats, response to CRS request, March 2011.

Note: This data reflect non-budget quality estimates of DOD counterdrug support provided or efforts in these countries/regions; DOD formal budget submissions to Congress do not measure counterdrug programs by countries/regions.

Table 7. U.S. Assistance for Crop Eradication, FY2007-FY2010 Est. (in current U.S. $).

	FY2007	FY2008	FY2009	FY2010 est.
Afghanistan	—	169,871,000	237,000,000	35,000,000
Bolivia	8,544,000	7,285,000	8,496,000	6,930,000
Colombia	159,208,000	137,880,000	—	109,050,000
Guatemala	200,000	200,000	270,000	22,000
Laos	—	145,000	—	—
Mexico	200,000	—	—	—
Pakistan	2,300,000	1,000,000	1,000,000	2,000,000
Peru	32,500,000	14,864,000	14,400,000	16,120,000
Western Hemisphere Regional	—	—	—	105,000
Total	202,952,000	331,245,000	261,166,000	169,227,000

Source: U.S. Department of State, Office of the Director of Foreign Assistance (F), response to CRS request, March 2011.

Note: Data included in this chart represent all State Department FY2008, FY2009, and FY2010 Operational Plan updates as of March 15, 2011 (0100 EST). In FY2007, plans were completed by all USAID offices except Iraq and by some State Department offices. FY 2009 GHCS-State and GHCS-USAID account values do not currently include funds reported in the COPRS system for the PEPFAR program.

Figure 5 and Table 6 summarize DOD estimates, provided to CRS, for DOD-funded counterdrug assistance to foreign countries, by region. Note that, unlike the State Department, DOD counternarcotics funding is not budgeted or allocated by country or region. In annual defense department appropriations, DOD has received department-wide funding for drug control efforts, both domestically and internationally, through a single central transfer account, called "Drug Interdiction and Counter-Drug Activities."

POLICY ISSUES

Over the years, U.S. counterdrug efforts have expanded to include a broad array of tools to attack the drug trade using several foreign policy approaches. Through its appropriations and federal oversight responsibilities, the 112th Congress may choose to evaluate current efforts, which appear to center around four main drug control policy strategies: (1) combating the production of drugs at the source, (2) combating the flow of drugs in transit, (3) dismantling illicit drug networks, and (4) creating incentives for international cooperation on drug control. The following sections describe and analyze each of these primary strategies and their legislative sources.

Combating the Production of Drugs at the Source

Major U.S. policy tools for combating the production of illicit drugs, particularly cocaine and heroin, center on the eradication of coca bush and opium poppy crops and the provision of alternative livelihood options to drug crop farmers. Both policy approaches ultimately seek to reduce the amount of illicit drug crops cultivated.

Crop Eradication

Eradication programs seek to combat the flow of plant-based illegal drugs at the root of the supply chain—in the fields where the crops are grown. Crop eradication can take several forms, including (1) aerial fumigation, which involves the spraying of fields with herbicide; (2) manual removal, which involves the physical up-rooting and destruction of crops; and (3) mechanical removal, which involves the use of tractors and all-terrain vehicles to harrow the fields. The United States supports programs to eradicate coca, opium, and marijuana in a number of countries, including primarily Colombia and

Afghanistan (see Table 7). These efforts are conducted by U.S. government agencies and contractors that administer U.S. eradication programs providing producer countries with support to eradicate drug crops with chemical herbicides, technical assistance, specialized equipment, and spray aircraft. In FY2009, the State Department spent approximately $432 million on international eradication programs.[54]

Eradication is a longstanding but controversial U.S. policy regarding international drug control. As recently as 2008, the State Department had considered crop control the "most cost-effective means of cutting supply," because drugs cannot enter the illegal trade if the crops were never planted, destroyed, or left unharvested.[55] Without drug cultivation, the State Department's rationale continued, "there would be no need for costly enforcement and interdiction operations." Proponents of eradication further argue that it is easier to locate and destroy crops in the field than to locate subsequently processed drugs on smuggling routes or on the streets of U.S. cities. Put differently, a kilogram of powder cocaine is far more difficult to detect than the 300 to 500 kilograms of coca leaf that are required to make that same kilogram. Also, because crops constitute the cheapest link in the narcotics chain, producers may devote fewer economic resources to prevent their detection than to conceal more expensive and refined forms of the drug product.

Opponents of expanded supply reduction policy generally question whether reduction of the foreign supply of narcotic drugs is achievable and whether it would have a meaningful impact on levels of illicit drug use in the United States. Manual eradication requires significant time and human resources, reportedly involving upward of 20 work-hours of effort to pull up and destroy one hectare of coca plants.[56] Aerial application of herbicide is not legal or feasible in many countries and is expensive to implement where it is permitted.[57] Aerial fumigation in Colombia has also raised allegations that the herbicide chemical used has caused negative human, animal, and environmental consequences.[58]

Others question whether a global policy of simultaneous crop control is cost-effective or politically feasible because eradication efforts may also potentially result in negative political, economic, and social consequences for the producing country, especially in conflict or post-conflict environments.[59] Some argue that this has been the case with respect to eradication efforts in Afghanistan, where some U.S. officials have acknowledged that poppy eradication may have caused many poor Afghan farmers to ally with insurgents and other enemies of the Afghan government.[60] In 2009, Richard

Holbrooke, who was the Obama Administration's Special Representative for Afghanistan and Pakistan at the time, called Western eradication policies in Afghanistan "a failure" and stated that they have "wasted hundreds and hundreds of millions of dollars."[61] Further, aerial eradication remains a high-risk activity, as spray planes and their crew are targeted by drug traffickers. In 2003, the Revolutionary Armed Forces of Colombia (FARC), which the State Department lists as a foreign terrorist organization, shot down a U.S. government plane in the Colombian jungle, killing the American pilot and a Colombian air force sergeant and taking three other crew members, all U.S. defense contractors, hostage.[62] They remained FARC hostages until July 2008.[63]

Table 8. U.S. Alternative Development Foreign Assistance, FY2007-FY2010 Est. (in current U.S. $).

Country	FY2007	FY2008	FY2009	FY2010 est.
Afghanistan	—	123,475,185	161,518,000	157,000,000
Bolivia	26,174,500	7,662,073	17,746,100	17,248,000
Colombia	57,533,000	108,857,000	109,831,000	101,021,000
Ecuador	8,194,957	2,269,000	7,737,000	10,449,000
Laos	—	300,000	100,000	—
Pakistan	—	—	—	2,000,000
Peru	42,864,500	21,917,000	31,645,000	27,221,000
TOTAL	134,766,957	274,480,258	328,577,100	314,939,000

Source: U.S. Department of State, Office of the Director of Foreign Assistance (F), response to CRS request, March 2011.

Note: Data included in this chart represent all State Department FY2008, FY2009, and FY2010 Operational Plan updates as of March 15, 2011 (0100 EST). In FY2007, plans were completed by all USAID offices except Iraq and by some State Department offices. FY2009 GHCS-State and GHCS-USAID account values do not currently include funds reported in the COPRS system for the PEPFAR program.

Alternative Development

U.S. counterdrug policy also includes foreign assistance specifically targeted to illicit drug crop farmers. Alternative development can be viewed as a form of drug crop eradication. The ultimate goal is to convince current farmers to abandon their drug crops and switch to licit, sustainable livelihoods and sources of income. Whereas other eradication methods involve the physical removal or chemical destruction of illicit drug crops, alternative development involves the introduction of crop substitution options, training in sustainable farming techniques, infrastructure development, and other projects that make alternative livelihoods economically more attractive. The U.S. government considers alternative development a key component to drug supply reduction policies and has active programs in Southeast Asia, Southwest Asia, and South America (see Table 8).

U.S. alternative development programs, funded and run mainly by the State Department and U.S. Agency for International Development (USAID), support U.S. counternarcotics objectives by helping countries develop economic alternatives to narcotics production, expand legal employment opportunities, and offer other incentives to farmers to discontinue planting illicit drug crops. In theory, this approach is designed to complement law enforcement and eradication efforts to provide both a "carrot and stick" strategy.

For several decades, alternative development has been implemented in various forms and with varying success.[64] Since the late 1960s, when alternative development policies were initially conceived as simply crop substitution projects, efforts have somewhat expanded to include a broader concept of alternative development. Current U.S. programs include not only crop substitution projects but also the development of and assistance for roads, infrastructure, and health care.

Some observers, however, claim that while current U.S. efforts often aim to achieve this broadened concept of alternative development, they may not always achieve it in practice. Some indicate that a relationship between alternative development projects and a reduction in illicit drug production may be tenuous, as policy coordination between alternative development projects and eradication and interdiction efforts remains limited in some cases.[65] Further, it appears that alternative development projects are not implemented in most regions where illicit crops are grown today. According to reports, approximately 10% to 15% of areas under illicit cultivation are covered by alternative development projects supported by the international community, and, on average, 5% of farmers of illicit crops receive alternative development assistance.[66] Common factors limiting the reach and prevalence of alternative development projects include ongoing security threats in areas of illicit crop cultivation, lack of political will or resources to administer alternative development projects, and local distrust of government or external influences.

Combating the Flow of Drugs in Transit

Interdiction efforts seek to combat the drug trade as traffickers begin moving drug products from source countries to their final destinations. The Department of Defense is the single lead federal agency for the detection and monitoring of aerial and maritime movement of illegal drugs toward the United States. Along with the Defense Department, several other U.S. federal agencies are involved in coordinating operations with foreign government interdiction forces and providing law enforcement training and other forms of assistance to foreign countries in order to deny drug traffickers the use of transit routes.

Within the so-called "transit zone"—a 42-million square-mile area between Central and South America and the U.S. southern borders, which covers the Caribbean Sea, the Gulf of Mexico, and the eastern Pacific Ocean—a DOD-led interagency group called the Joint Inter-Agency Task Force South (JIATF-South) coordinates interdiction operations across federal agency participants, as well as international liaisons from Great Britain, France, the Netherlands, and several Latin American countries. The U.S.-Mexican border is the primary point of entry for cocaine shipments and other drugs smuggled into the United States.[67]

Outside the transit zone, other international interdiction operations involving U.S. agencies, mainly DEA, include Operation Containment, Project Cohesion, and Project Prism. Operation Containment, a multinational law enforcement effort established in 2002 and led by DEA, aims to place a "security belt" around Afghanistan to prevent processing chemicals for converting opium poppy to heroin from entering the country and opium and heroin from leaving.[68] Project Cohesion, an international precursor chemical control initiative established in 2005 and led by the International Narcotics Control Board (INCB),[69] tracks precursor chemicals involved in the production of cocaine and heroin. Project Prism, a U.N.-sponsored initiative, monitors and controls illicit trade in precursor chemicals used in the production of amphetamine-type synthetic drugs. The Obama Administration's revised 2010 counternarcotics policy for Afghanistan also emphasizes in particular interdiction and the dismantling of Afghan drug trafficking syndicates.[70]

INTERNATIONAL DRUG FLOW ATTACK STRATEGY

As part of U.S. law enforcement efforts to combat the flow of drugs and related illicit movements of cash and laundered drug proceeds, DEA developed the International Drug Flow Attack Strategy (DFAS) in mid-2005. The goal of the strategy is to disrupt cocaine movements between the source zones in Latin America and the United States through intelligence-led operations that are coordinated with foreign law enforcement counterparts in source zones, transit zones, and arrival zones. Although descriptions of many aspects of the DFAS initiative are not available publicly, the State Department reports that Operation All Inclusive, a multi-year counterdrug law enforcement operation in the Western Hemisphere, has been one of the primary efforts implementing DFAS techniques and tools. From January 2008 through September 2008, Operation All Inclusive netted more than 100 metric tons of cocaine, 225 kilograms of heroin, 140 metric tons of marijuana, $92 million in drug proceeds, and 1,278 arrests.

Several U.S. agencies also provide foreign law enforcement training and assistance in order to enhance interdiction efforts abroad. The Department of State, the U.S. Coast Guard, U.S. Customs and Border Protection, and DEA are involved in providing anti-narcotics law enforcement training, technical assistance, and equipment for foreign personnel. The U.S. military provides international support for drug monitoring and detection. In addition, the United States regularly contributes funding and expertise to law enforcement assistance activities of the United Nations and other international organizations.

U.S. interdiction activities in the transit zone, spanning the continental and maritime border areas between the United States and Latin America and the Caribbean, are sometimes considered among the bright spots of U.S. counterdrug efforts. The State Department reports that its interdiction activities in the Caribbean, including Operation Bahamas Turks and Caicos (OPBAT), contributed to a drop in illegal drug flows from 70% in the 1980s to less than 10% in recent years.[71] A 2005 report released by the Government Accountability Office (GAO), for example, highlighted the role of improved interagency coordination and international cooperation for improvements in transit zone interdiction operations.[72] Drug trafficking organizations, however, are reportedly growing increasingly sophisticated in their evasion techniques, and some observers are concerned that current interdiction capabilities may not be sufficient for long-term reductions in drug supplies. Proponents of strong drug interdiction policies, for example, have long been concerned that the nation's focus on anti-terror objectives will detract from resources and political will needed to combat foreign illicit drug production and trafficking. Supporting such concerns, the 2005 GAO report states that the commitment of U.S. military assets to Iraq and Afghanistan in the 2000s may have hampered the ability of U.S. law enforcement to intercept drug shipments in the future.

Table 9. U.S. Civilian Assistance for Interdiction, FY2007-FY2010 Est.

Country	FY2007	FY2008	FY2009	FY2010 est.
Afghanistan	—	14,622,000	21,000,000	254,879,000
Argentina	—	70,000	85,000	275,000
Bolivia	20,696,000	18,138,000	12,688,000	8,270,000
Brazil	—	833,000	300,000	200,000
Cape Verde	—	496,000	500,000	723,000
Colombia	113,612,000	99,248,000	—	83,900,000
Dominican Republic	—	150,000	3,250,000	1,750,000
Eastern Caribbean	—	—	230,000	—
Ecuador	—	6,143,000	6,359,000	2,550,000
El Salvador	—	200,000	—	—
Georgia	—	300,000	150,000	200,000
Ghana	—	496,000	500,000	500,000
Guatemala	840,000	1,140,000	1,610,000	1,056,000
Guinea	—	—	50,000	—
Guinea-Bissau	—	—	—	1,500,000
Haiti	1,010,000	1,350,000	2,835,000	—
Honduras	—	608,400	—	—
Indonesia	500,000	500,000	500,000	500,000
Jamaica	—	250,000	150,000	—
Kazakhstan	—	316,000	204,000	180,000
Kyrgyz Republic	—	775,000	547,000	—
Laos	—	365,000	300,000	300,000

Table 9. (Continued)

Country	FY2007	FY2008	FY2009	FY2010 est.
Mexico	12,916,000	18,908,000	144,200,000	75,000,000
Morocco	—	—	—	750,000
Mozambique	—	—	—	300,000
Nicaragua	—	500,000	—	—
Nigeria	—	450,000	60,000	250,000
Pakistan	700,000	1,000,000	2,000,000	2,000,000
Panama	—	770,000	600,000	—
Paraguay	—	278,000	215,000	500,000
Peru	14,807,000	17,132,000	18,500,000	19,325,000
Philippines	100,000	—	—	—
Tajikistan	—	—	1,300,000	1,350,000
The Bahamas	—	—	150,000	—
Trans-Sahara Counter- Terrorism Partnership	—	—	—	2,000,000
Trinidad and Tobago	—	177,000	230,000	—
Turkey	—	25,000	235,000	—
Turkmenistan	—	—	145,000	175,000
Western Hemisphere Regional	—	—	6,000,000	25,862,000
TOTAL	165,181,000	185,853,880	225,364,000	505,045,000

Source: U.S. Department of State, Office of the Director of Foreign Assistance (F), response to CRS request, March 2011.

Note: Data included in this chart represent all State Department FY2008, FY2009, and FY2010 Operational Plan updates as of March 15, 2011 (0100 EST). In FY2007, plans were completed by all USAID offices except Iraq and by some State Department offices. FY2009 GHCS-State and GHCS-USAID account values do not currently include funds reported in the COPRS system for the PEPFAR program.

Some observers, however, caution that interdiction efforts could raise the retail price of illegal drugs, potentially resulting in a perverse incentive that actually increases the economic rewards to drug traffickers; interdiction efforts that appear to be reaping success in dismantling major drug trafficking networks may nevertheless pose the unintended consequence of sparking short-term increases in drug trafficking-related violence, as surviving drug traffickers compete with one another for control—often violently—of drug routes. This appears to have been in part a contributing factor to the ongoing drug-related violence in Mexico—and some observers are raising the concern that similar consequences may occur in Afghanistan under the Obama Administration's renewed emphasis on interdiction efforts to combat the Afghan opiate trade.[73]

Dismantling Transnational Drug Networks

Key U.S. foreign policy tools available for targeting major drug traffickers and their illicit networks include establishing extradition agreements with foreign countries, freezing and blocking foreign criminal assets within U.S. jurisdiction, and building foreign capacity to investigate, arrest, prosecute, and incarcerate drug traffickers domestically.

Extradition to the United States

The U.S. government regularly uses extradition as an important judicial tool against suspected drug traffickers located abroad. Extradition refers to the formal surrender of a person by a state to another state for prosecution. Proponents of extradition to the United States argue that suspected criminals are more likely to receive a fair trial in U.S. courts than in countries where the local judicial process may be corrupt and where suspects can use bribes and intimidation to manipulate the outcome of a trial.

STATE DEPARTMENT NARCOTICS REWARDS PROGRAM

Through the Narcotics Rewards Program, the State Department offers up to $5 million for information leading to the arrest or conviction of certain major drug traffickers.[74] Currently, the State Department is offering rewards for information associated with 40 at-large foreign drug traffickers, Mexican and Colombian traffickers. According to the State Department, rewards have been paid for assistance in the capture of at least nine previously listed drug traffickers.

U.S. bilateral judicial cooperation with Mexico and Colombia is often cited as particularly exemplary, yielding record numbers of extradited traffickers to the United States.[75] In 2010, Mexico extradited 94 individuals to the United States. Colombia extradited 186 to the United States in 2009, yielding a total of more than 1,041 individuals since 1997, when Colombia's legislature enacted a non-retroactive law to formalize U.S.-Colombian extradition cooperation.

Some anecdotal evidence appears to suggest that the threat of extradition has affected the behavior of foreign drug trafficking organizations. For example, some Colombian drug traffickers are reportedly distancing themselves from overt drug distribution activities, which could be used as evidence to trigger extradition. Nevertheless, this counterdrug tool remains controversial and is not universally supported. Many countries simply refuse to extradite drug traffickers, citing concerns about the potential use of the death penalty in the United States against its citizens and state sovereignty rights. Burma is one such country, which continues to refuse to extradite four suspected drug traffickers under indictment in the United States. Some observers claim that suspected traffickers often take advantage of such limitations in the extradition system and seek safe haven in countries that are unwilling to extradite.

Freezing and Blocking Foreign Criminal Assets

To reap the financial benefits of the illegal drug trade, traffickers must launder their illicit profits into the licit economy. As a result, the United States and other members of the international community have sought to use anti-money laundering efforts as a tool to combat this upstream activity in the illegal drug market. Currently, several U.S. agencies are involved in international anti-money laundering efforts designed to enhance financial transaction transparency and regulation, improve cooperation and coordination with foreign governments and private financial institutions, and provide foreign countries with law enforcement training and support.

Congress has been active in pursuing anti-money laundering regulations and program oversight. In 1999, Congress passed the Foreign Narcotics Kingpin Designation Act to authorize the President to target the financial profits that significant foreign narcotics traffickers and their organizations (known as "Specially Designated Narcotics Trafficker Kingpins," or SDNTKs) have accumulated from their illicit activities.[76] This tool seeks to deny SDNTKs and their related businesses access to the U.S. financial system and all trade transactions involving U.S. companies and individuals.[77]

Following the September 11, 2001, terrorist attacks, Congress further strengthened U.S. measures to combat money laundering by providing the Secretary of the Treasury with new authorities to impose a set of regulatory restrictions, or "special measures," against foreign jurisdictions, foreign financial institutions, and certain classes of financial transactions involving foreign jurisdictions, if deemed by the Treasury Secretary to be "of primary money laundering concern."[78] These anti-money laundering tools are designed not only to address drug trafficking, but also to combat other forms of related criminal activity, including terrorist financing.

In addition, Congress requires that the State Department include in its annual International Narcotics Control Strategy Report (INCSR) a separate volume devoted to the state of international money laundering and financial crimes in each country. Among the report's congressionally mandated requirements, the State Department annually identifies the world's "major money laundering countries," defined as those countries "whose financial institutions engage in currency transactions involving significant amounts of proceeds from international narcotics trafficking" and other serious crimes (see Figure 6).

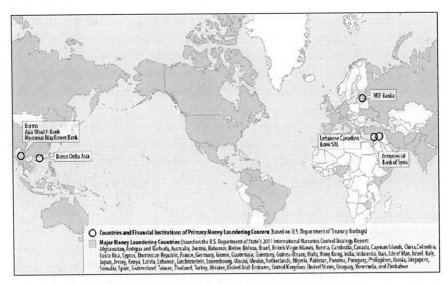

Sources: U.S. Department of State, *2011 INCSR*; U.S. Department of the Treasury, Financial Crimes Enforcement Network, Section 311 Special Measures, at http://www.fincen.gov/statutes_regs/patriot/section311.html.

Figure 6. Major Money Laundering Countries and Jurisdictions of Primary Money Laundering Concern.

U.S. officials and some observers have highlighted the value of anti-money laundering efforts in combating drug trafficking. In 2007, the Treasury Department's Office of Foreign Assets Control (OFAC) reported that anti-money laundering efforts against Colombian drug cartels have been effective in isolating and incapacitating designated supporters, businesses, and front companies linked to the Cali Cartel and Norte del Valle Cartel.[79] Some observers also describe the Treasury Secretary's additional authorities to designate jurisdictions of primary money laundering concern and apply "special measures" against these jurisdictions as having "potentially profound effects on the financial services industry."[80] Treasury's designation of Banco Delta Asia, for example, successfully resulted in the freezing of some $25 million in North Korean assets—funds that reportedly included counterfeit U.S. currency and profits from other North Korean criminal activity, including drug trafficking.[81]

Skeptics of the use of anti-money laundering efforts to combat drug trafficking argue that tracking illicit financial transactions may be more difficult and may yield less success than other counterdrug tools.[82] As the State Department's 2008 money laundering and financial crimes report reveals, major challenges in tracking and disrupting international money laundering activities remain.[83] The same types of money laundering methods—bulk cash smuggling, trade-based money laundering, and others— that the State Department identified as issues of concern more than a decade ago remain among the most used forms of money laundering today. Further, emerging challenges include the growing volume of financial transactions, especially the volume of international electronic transfers, and the movement of illegal money laundering outside formal banking channels, including through "hawala"-type chains of transnational money brokers and through the use of stored-value cards.

Building Foreign Law Enforcement Capacity

Another element of U.S. efforts to dismantle foreign drug networks involves providing foreign countries with the tools also improve their domestic efforts to dismantle drug networks. Such assistance, in the form of training, equipping, and other institutional capacity building, ultimately seeks to strengthen foreign judicial and law enforcement institutions and assist in developing host nation administrative infrastructures to combat the illicit drug trade. Institutional development programs focus mainly on fighting corruption and training to support criminal justice system reforms and the rule of law. A variety of U.S. agencies are involved in counterdrug-related capacity building efforts abroad, including the State Department, USAID, the Department of Justice, and the Department of Defense.

According to the State Department, drug trafficking organizations often seek to subvert or co-opt governments in order to guarantee a secure operating environment and essentially "buy their way into power."[84] Anti-corruption efforts thus seek to prevent traffickers from undermining the legitimacy and effectiveness of foreign government institutions. Some observers, however, argue that counterdrug policies are placing too little emphasis on projects that help foreign countries develop a culture supportive of the rule of law. One expert explained in congressional testimony in 2007, "unless foreign police organizations recognize and internalize what the rule of law means, what its key characteristics are, and why the rule of law is necessary to accomplish their mission, no amount of aid will get the job done."[85]

Creating Incentives for International Cooperation

Congress has historically played a major role in developing counternarcotics-related legislative conditions on U.S. foreign assistance and unilateral trade preference programs.

DEFINING THE DRUG MAJORS

A "major illicit drug producing country" is statutorily defined in Sec. 481 of the Foreign Assistance Act of 1961 (FAA), as amended (22 U.S.C. 2291(e)(2)), as a country in which:

- (a) 1,000 hectares of more of illicit opium poppy is cultivated or harvested during a year;
- (b) 1,000 hectares or more of illicit coca is cultivated or harvested during a year; or
- (c) 5,000 hectares or more of illicit cannabis is cultivated or harvested during a year, unless the President determines that such illicit cannabis production does not significantly affect the United States.

A "major drug transit country" is statutorily defined in Sec. 481 of the FAA, as amended (22 U.S.C. 2291(e)(5)), as a country

- (a) in which there is a significant direct source of illicit narcotic or psychotropic drugs or other controlled substances significantly affecting the United States; or
- (b) through which such drugs or substances are transported.

Conditions on Foreign Aid

In an effort to deter foreign governments from aiding or participating in illicit drug production or trafficking, the President may suspend U.S. foreign assistance appropriations to countries that are major illegal drug producers or major transit countries for illegal drugs, known as "drug majors."[86] For FY2011, the President has identified 20 drug majors (see Figure 7). Of these, Congress requires that the President certify that the drug majors have not "failed demonstrably" to make at least "substantial efforts" to adhere to their obligations during the previous year under international counternarcotics agreements.

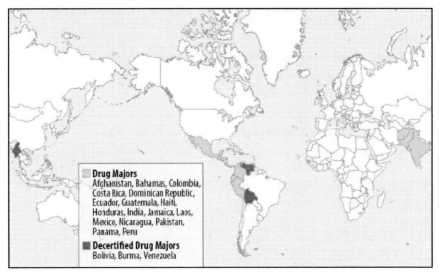

Source: Barack Obama, Presidential Determination No. 2010-16, "Memorandum to the Secretary of State: Major Drug Transit or Major Illicit Drug Producing Countries for Fiscal Year 2011," September 2010.

Figure 7. Map of World Drug Majors in FY2011.

Failure to receive a presidential certification of substantial counternarcotics efforts may result in certain foreign assistance prohibitions against those drug majors. Decertified drug majors may continue to receive U.S. foreign assistance, however, if the President determines that assistance is "vital" to U.S. national interests. Alternatively, foreign assistance to drug majors countries may nevertheless be withheld by Congress, despite a presidential certification, if Congress enacts a joint resolution disapproving of the President's certification.

For FY2011, the President did not certify three drug majors—Bolivia, Burma, and Venezuela. However, for two of the three countries, Bolivia and Venezuela, the President partially waived the aid sanctions, permitting the U.S. government to provide assistance to Venezuela for "limited programs" and to Bolivia for "continued support for bilateral programs" (see Figure 7).[87]

Since its creation in 1986, the drug majors designation process has garnered significant controversy. Supporters of the process argue that, overall, it is an "effective diplomatic instrument" to enforce international drug control commitments because it holds foreign governments "publicly responsible for their actions before their international peers."[88] However, in a few extreme cases, the drug majors designation does not appear to have much effect on a country's drug control policies. In the case of Bolivia's designation in 2008, the policy appears to have had the opposite effect, in part causing a further rift in counternarcotics policy between Bolivia and the United States.[89] Observers from many countries criticize the unilateral and noncooperative nature of the drug certification requirements; such critics recommend moving toward multilateral and regional fora for evaluating governments' counterdrug efforts. Others question the extent to which the process reduces the scope of the illegal drug trade, when many of the world's drug producers and transit areas are located in countries that are not designated as drug majors or decertified by the President. Some have suggested the OAS/CICAD Multilateral Evaluation Mechanism (MEM), a regional system of peer review on drug control policies in OAS countries, could serve as an alternative model to facilitate international drug control cooperation.[90]

CONGRESSIONAL ROLE IN DRUG CERTIFICATION PROCEDURES

When making the annual drug majors decisions, the President may choose from two legislatively mandated methods available. One is codified at 22 U.S.C. 2291j while the second is codified at 22 U.S.C. 2291j-1.

The Original Certification Procedure: 22 U.S.C. 2291j

Beginning 1986 (P.L. 99-570), Congress required that the President determine and certify to Congress that major illicit drug producing or drug transit countries (i.e., drug majors) were "fully cooperating" with the U.S. government to combat the illegal drug trade. 22 U.S.C. 2291j requires that 50% of certain bilateral assistance be withheld and that the U.S. government oppose multilateral development assistance to the drug majors until the President makes his determinations and certifications.[91] If the President does not determine and certify a drug major as having met the "fully cooperating" requirement (or if Congress enacts a joint resolution disapproving of a Presidential certification), then the President must decide which of the two following actions will take place:

- **U.S. Denial of Assistance:** 100% of bilateral assistance is prohibited from being obligated and the U.S. government continues to oppose multilateral development assistance until the country is eligible for certification; or
- **Continuance of All or a Portion of Aid for National Interest Reasons:** Aid continues, not because the country qualifies for certification, but because the President determines that "the vital national interests of the United States require that the assistance withheld ... be provided." In this scenario, multilateral development assistance could also be supported.

The Revised Drug Majors Process: 22 U.S.C. 2291j-1

While not eliminating the certification procedures under 22 U.S.C. 2291j, the Foreign Operations, Export Financing, and Related Programs Appropriations Act, 2002 (P.L. 107-115), temporarily allowed for the suspension of the prior certification procedures and their replacement with a new set of procedures. The Foreign Relations Authorization Act, Fiscal Year 2003 (P.L. 107-228), made permanent the modified certification requirement under P.L. 107-115, and this new requirement became codified under 22 U.S.C. 2291j-1.

In lieu of following the original certification procedures (22 U.S.C. 2291j), the revised drug majors process (22 U.S.C. 2291j-1) required the President to designate and withhold assistance from only the worst offending drug majors—those that were determined by the President as having "failed demonstrably" to make substantial efforts to combat illicit drugs. It also eliminated the requirement to withhold initially 50% of bilateral aid prior to the President's designation and certification to Congress.

The change in standards from whether a country had "cooperated fully" to whether it had "failed demonstrably" effectively shifted the "burden of proof to an assumption that foreign nations were cooperating with the United States and had to be proved otherwise to trigger the restrictions" in foreign assistance.[92] For those countries that were designated as having failed demonstrably, the same two options remained as under 22 U.S.C. 2291j: (1) 100% denial of U.S. bilateral and multilateral assistance or (2) continuance of all or a portion of aid for national interest reasons.

Methamphetamine Precursor Chemicals

An additional certification process was enacted by Congress as part of the Combat Methamphetamine Epidemic Act of 2005.[93] This law amends the Foreign Assistance Act of 1961 to require the State Department to report the five largest importing and exporting countries of two precursor drugs, ephedrine and pseudoephedrine, commonly used to produce methamphetamine, and certify whether these countries are fully cooperating with the United States on methamphetamine chemical precursor control. Nations deemed not to be fully cooperating face a loss of U.S. bilateral assistance and U.S. opposition to multilateral assistance in the multilateral development banks.[94] For FY2010, the State Department identified 16 major precursor chemical source countries: Argentina, Belgium, Brazil, Canada, Chile, China, Germany, India, Mexico, the Netherlands, Singapore, South Korea, Taiwan, Thailand, the United Kingdom, and the United States. So far, the President has not decertified any country for its efforts to control methamphetamine precursor chemicals.

Other Drug-Related Foreign Aid Certification Requirements

Several additional drug-related certification requirements have appeared in recent appropriations legislation for specific countries. While not codified certifications processes, failure to be certified under these provisions can result in the prohibition of various amounts of foreign aid. For example, since 2006, Congress has placed conditions on a portion of U.S. economic assistance to Afghanistan (the amount varies in appropriations legislation for different fiscal years) by requiring the President to certify that the Afghan government is "cooperating fully" with counternarcotics efforts prior to the obligation of funds, or to issue a national security waiver in order to allow assistance to continue even when counternarcotics cooperation does not reach the cooperating fully standard.[95] For each year, the President has issued a national security waiver.[96] For Mexico in FY2009 and FY2010, for example, 15% of U.S. aid for counternarcotics efforts is similarly contingent on a certification that human rights complaints and violations, which have reportedly increased from 182 in 2006 to 1,230 in 2008 as counternarcotics efforts have been ramped up, are addressed.[97]

Eligibility for Trade Preference Programs

In 1991, Congress passed the Andean Trade Preference Act (ATPA; P.L. 102-182). Congress later renewed and expanded the program in the 2002 Andean Trade Promotion and Drug Eradication Act (ATPDEA; P.L. 107-210).[98] The ATPA and subsequent amendments have permitted select beneficiary countries in South America to export certain products to the United States duty-free or at otherwise preferential trade levels.[99]

One of the purposes of the ATPA has been to support, in part, broader U.S. international counterdrug policy. By reducing the costs associated with exporting legitimate goods to the United States, ATPA would theoretically provide an incentive for drug-producing countries in South America to switch to economically viable alternative sources of income. In addition, pursuant to the ATPA, one of the eligibility criteria for renewed benefits under the Act is whether the beneficiary countries have upheld their international, regional, and bilateral commitments to combat drugs.[100] (See Table 10 on the status of ATPA beneficiary countries.)

Table 10. Status of ATPA Beneficiary Countries.

Beneficiary Country	Date of Presidential Proclamation Designating Beneficiary Countries	Date When Beneficiary Status Went into Effect	Date When Beneficiary Status was Suspended (if applicable)	Date When Beneficiary Expired or is Set to Expire in Law
Bolivia	July 2, 1992 (Presidential Proclamation No. 6456; 57 FR 30097)	effective July 22, 1992	October 1, 2008 (73 FR 57158) a	June 30, 2009
Colombia	July 2, 1992 (Presidential Proclamation No. 6455; 57 FR 30069)	effective July 22, 1992	N/A	February 12, 2011
Ecuador	April 13, 1993 (Presidential Proclamation No. 6544; 58 FR 19547)	effective April 30, 1993	N/A	February 12, 2011
Peru	August 11, 1993 (Presidential Proclamation No. 6585; 58 FR 43239)	effective August 26, 1993	N/A	December 31, 2010b

Source: CRS summary of the ATPA, as amended, and *Federal Register* (FR) notices.

a. Bolivia has been suspended from the ATPA trade preference program because it failed to meet one of the eligibility requirements for the program. Specifically, it failed demonstrably, during the previous 12 months, to make substantial efforts to uphold its international commitment to combat drugs. Its suspension in December 2008, in effect, suspended trade preferences. In June 2009, the time period expired for the President to re-designate Bolivia as a beneficiary country.

b. The ATPA trade preferences were not renewed because Peru has entered into a free trade agreement with the United States, which was implemented in February 2009.

A longstanding issue of debate, however, has been the extent to which the ATPA has been effective in providing Andean coca farmers alternative livelihoods and ultimately reducing illicit coca cultivation. As required by the ATPA legislation, the United States International Trade Commission (USITC) submits to Congress a biennial report that includes, among other matters, an analysis of the effectiveness of the ATPA/ATPDEA in "promoting drug-related crop eradication and crop substitution efforts of the beneficiary countries."[101] The last report was issued in September 2010, evaluating the 2008-2009 time period, concluding, as the USITC has in previous years, that "the effectiveness of ATPA in reducing illicit coca cultivation and promoting crop substitution efforts in the Andean countries continues to be small and mostly indirect."[102]

CONCLUSION

Many observers highlight the importance of international drug control policy, particularly because of the transnational nature of the drug trade, whereas others continue to criticize existing policies and mechanisms for failing to achieve sufficient progress in combating illegal drugs.[103] The UNODC has reported in recent years that global drug use has stabilized, on average; global opium poppy and coca cultivation is in decline; and global illicit drug seizures are up—and that a major contributing factor has been the continued international support for drug control policies.[104] Global coordination, many say, is vital for lasting success in combating the international drug trade. At the same time, however, others criticize the international drug control system for failing to achieve the United Nation's stated goal of "eliminating or reducing significantly" by 2008 the production and availability of synthetic drugs and precursors, as well as the cultivation of the coca bush, cannabis plant, and opium poppy.[105] In 2009, the U.N.'s Commission on Narcotic Drugs set a new date of 2019 to "eliminate or reduce significantly and measurably" the cultivation of illegal plant-based drugs, the demand for illegal drugs, the production and trafficking of synthetic drugs, the diversion and trafficking of precursor chemicals used in the manufacture of illegal drugs, and drug-related money laundering.[106]

The 112th Congress may continue to exercise its oversight and assess existing U.S. international drug policy. Emerging questions in the drug policy debate include the following:

- In what ways are counternarcotics strategies facilitating or driving recent increases in drug trafficking-related violence? Are spikes in drug-related violence common or inevitable consequences of heightened counternarcotics operations? In what ways might governments mitigate or dampen current and potentially future increases in drug-related violence?
- How do counternarcotics policies interact with counterterrorism, counterinsurgency, and anti-money laundering priorities, particularly in countries such as Afghanistan, where the U.S. government may have an interest in all three issues?
- What role should the Department of Defense play in providing foreign counternarcotics assistance?
- How should U.S. policymakers weigh the benefits of aerial eradication as a counternarcotics policy tool with the social, financial, and political costs it may incur?
- To what extent is it a common phenomenon that human rights are violated over the course of drug-related investigations and operations? In what ways might human rights violations undermine or threaten drug control policies?
- To what extent should U.S. counternarcotics policy take into account economic development, social development, and health and harm reduction programs, and are such efforts sufficiently coordinated with international and bilateral partners?
- How do counternarcotics policies interact with related foreign policy goals of anti-corruption, justice sector reform, and improving the rule of law?
- How might international regulatory and legal constraints limit the reach of U.S. counternarcotics policy and potentially offer drug syndicates foreign safe havens? What legislative options might be available to prevent such legal safe havens from existing?

APPENDIX A. COMPARISON OF DRUG DATA, BY COUNTRY, 2005-2009

Drug Crop Cultivation Estimates

Opium Poppy Cultivation

Table A-1. Afghanistan: Comparison of Opium Poppy Cultivation Estimates 2005-2009.

	2005	2006	2007	2008	2009	2010
United Nations	104,000	165,000	193,000	157,000	123,000	n/a
United States	107,400	172,600	202,000	157,000	131,000	119,000

Source: U.N. Office on Drugs and Crime (UNODC), *World Drug Report* (2010), p. 138; U.S. Department of State, Bureau for International Narcotics and Law Enforcement Affairs, International Narcotics Control Strategy Report, Vol. 1 (2011), p. 21.

Notes: U.N. source is the National Illicit Crop Monitoring System, which is supported by UNODC.

Table A-2. Burma: Comparison of Opium Poppy Cultivation Estimates 2005-2009.

	2005	2006	2007	2008	2009
United Nations	32,800	21,500	27,700	28,500	31,700
United States	40,000	21,000	21,700	22,500	17,000

Source: U.N. Office on Drugs and Crime (UNODC), *World Drug Report* (2010), p. 138; U.S. Department of State, Bureau for International Narcotics and Law Enforcement Affairs, International Narcotics Control Strategy Report, Vol. 1 (2011), p. 21.

Notes: U.N. source is the National Illicit Crop Monitoring System, which is supported by UNODC.

Table A-3. Colombia: Comparison of Opium Poppy Cultivation Estimates 2005-2009.

	2005	2006	2007	2008	2009
United Nations	1,950	1,023	715	394	356
United States	n.a.	2,300	1,000	n.a.	1,100

Source: U.N. Office on Drugs and Crime (UNODC), *World Drug Report* (2010), p. 138; U.S. Department of State, Bureau for International Narcotics and Law Enforcement Affairs, International Narcotics Control Strategy Report, Vol. 1 (2011), p. 21.

Notes: U.N. source is the Government of Colombia. In 2005, the U.S. government did not conduct a survey due to cloud cover. Partial surveys were conducted by the U.S. government in 2007 and 2009 due to cloud cover. The U.S. government did not conduct a survey in 2008.

Table A-4. Laos: Comparison of Opium Poppy Cultivation Estimates 2005-2009.

	2005	2006	2007	2008	2009
United Nations	1,800	2,500	1,500	1,600	1,900
United States	5,600	1,700	1,100	1,900	1,000

Source: U.N. Office on Drugs and Crime (UNODC), *World Drug Report* (2010), p. 138; U.S. Department of State, Bureau for International Narcotics and Law Enforcement Affairs, International Narcotics Control Strategy Report, Vol. 1 (2010), p. 23.

Notes: U.N. source is the National Illicit Crop Monitoring System, which is supported by UNODC. In 2009, the U.S. government conducted a partial survey of only the Phongsali growing area.

Table A-5. Mexico: Comparison of Opium Poppy Cultivation Estimates 2005-2009.

	2005	2006	2007	2008	2009
United Nations	3,300	5,000	6,900	15,000	n/a
United States	3,300	5,000	6,900	15,000	19,500

Source: U.N. Office on Drugs and Crime (UNODC), *World Drug Report* (2010), p. 138; U.S. Department of State, Bureau for International Narcotics and Law Enforcement Affairs, International Narcotics Control Strategy Report, Vol. 1 (2011), p. 21.

Notes: U.N. source is the U.S. government.

Coca Bush Cultivation

Table A-6. Bolivia: Comparison of Coca Bush Cultivation Estimates
2005-2009.

	2005	2006	2007	2008	2009
United Nations	25,400	27,500	28,900	30,500	30,900
United States	26,500	25,800	29,500	32,000	35,000

Source: U.N. Office on Drugs and Crime (UNODC), *World Drug Report* (2010), p.
162; U.S. Department of State, Bureau for International Narcotics and Law
Enforcement Affairs, International Narcotics Control Strategy Report, Vol. 1
(2011), p. 21.

Notes: U.N. sources through 2002 included the Inter-American Drug Abuse Control
Commission and the U.S. government. Since 2002 for the Yungas region and for
all regions of Bolivia since 2003, estimates were conducted by the National Illicit
Crop Monitoring System, supported by the UNODC.

Table A-7. Colombia: Comparison of Coca Bush Cultivation Estimates
2005-2009.

	2005	2006	2007	2008	2009
United Nations	86,000	78,000	99,000	81,000	68,000
United States	144,000	157,200	167,000	119,000	116,000

Source: U.N. Office on Drugs and Crime (UNODC), *World Drug Report* (2010), p.
162; U.S. Department of State, Bureau for International Narcotics and Law
Enforcement Affairs, International Narcotics Control Strategy Report, Vol. 1
(2011), p. 21.

Notes: U.N. source is the National Illicit Crop Monitoring System, which is supported
by UNODC.

Table A-8. Peru: Comparison of Coca Bush Cultivation Estimates
2005-2009.

	2005	2006	2007	2008	2009
United Nations	48,200	51,400	53,700	56,100	59,900
United States	34,000	42,000	36,000	41,000	40,000

Source: U.N. Office on Drugs and Crime (UNODC), *World Drug Report* (2010), p.
162; U.S. Department of State, Bureau for International Narcotics and Law
Enforcement Affairs, International Narcotics Control Strategy Report, Vol. 1
(20101), p. 21.

Notes: U.N. source is the National Illicit Crop Monitoring System, which is supported
by UNODC.

End Notes

[1] With few exceptions, the production and sale of controlled substances is legally permitted only if used for medical and scientific purposes.

[2] U.N. Office on Drugs and Crime (UNODC), *World Drug Report* (2010), p. 162.

[3] U.N. Office on Drugs and Crime (UNODC), *World Drug Report* (2010), p. 138.

[4] Ecstasy is the popular term for 3,4-methylenedioxmethamphetamine (MDMA).

[5] U.N. Office on Drugs and Crime (UNODC), *World Drug Report* (2010), p. 203.

[6] U.N. Office on Drugs and Crime (UNODC), *World Drug Report* (2010), p. 123.

[7] There is no universal definition for "problem drug user." U.N. data are based on information submitted by Member States to the United Nations and variously includes regular or frequent drug users deemed dependent on drug use and suffering from social and health consequences as a result of their drug use. U.N. Office on Drugs and Crime (UNODC), *World Drug Report* (2010), p. 125.

[8] U.N. Office on Drugs and Crime (UNODC), *World Drug Report* (2010), p. 5.

[9] According to the study, there are between 11 and 21.2 million drug-injecting users, of which between 0.8 and 6.6 million may be living with HIV. Total global estimates of people living with HIV are between 30 and 36 million. Bradley M. Mathers et al., "HIV Prevention, Treatment, and Care Services for People Who Inject Drugs: A Systematic Review of Global, Regional, and National Coverage," *The Lancet*, vol. 375, no. 9719 (March 20-26, 2010), pp. 1014-1028.

[10] U.S. Department of Justice, National Drug Intelligence Center, National Drug Threat Assessment 2010, No. 2010-Q0317-001, February 2010. Note also that the National Drug Threat Assessment defines drug "cartels." Specifically, it defines drug cartels to be "large, highly sophisticated organizations composed of multiple DTOs and cells with specific assignments such as drug transportation, security/enforcement, or money laundering. Drug cartel command-and-control structures are based outside the United States; however, they produce, transport, and distribute illicit drugs domestically with the assistance of DTOs that are either a part of or in an alliance with the cartel."

[11] See for example, Cornelius Graubner, *Drugs and Conflict: How the Mutual Impact of Illicit Drug Economies and Violent Conflict Influences Sustainable Development, Peace and Stability*, 2007.

[12] U.S. Embassy Kabul, U.S. Forces Afghanistan, *United States Government Integrated Civilian-Military Campaign Plan for Support to Afghanistan*, August 10, 2009.

[13] Examples include the shooting down of a drug eradication plane in Colombia in 1993, which resulted in the immediate shooting of the pilot and the taking hostage of three American defense contractors; the killing of five U.S. Drug Enforcement Administration (DEA) agents in Peru during the shooting down of a plane on a drug reconnaissance mission; and the torture and murder of DEA undercover agent Enrique "Kiki" Camarena Salazar in Mexico in 1985. Most recently, Immigration and Customs Enforcement (ICE) Special Agent Jaime Zapata was killed in February 2011 in northern Mexico by suspected drug traffickers. Another ICE agent was wounded in the same incident.

[14] See CRS Report R41075, *Southwest Border Violence: Issues in Identifying and Measuring Spillover Violence*, coordinated by Kristin M. Finklea.

[15] James R. Clapper, Director of National Intelligence, Statement for the Record on the Worldwide Threat Assessment of the U.S. Intelligence Community for the House Permanent Select Committee on Intelligence, February 10, 2011, and for the Senate Select Committee on Intelligence, February 16, 2011, available at http://www.dni.gov/testimonies/20110210_testimony_clapper.pdf.

[16] p. 215, UNODC, *2008 World Drug Report*, June 2008,available at http://daccessdds.un.org/doc/UNDOC/GEN/N98/775/09/PDF/

N9877509.pdf?OpenElement; UN Commission on Drugs, Report on the 52nd Session, E/2009/28, E/CN.7/2009/12 (2009), p. 44.

[17] Ibid, p. 217.

[18] See for example Vienna NGO Committee on Narcotic Drugs, "Beyond 2008 Declaration," July 9, 2008; available at http://www.vngoc.org/images/uploads/file/BEYOND%202008%20DECLARATION%20AND%20RESOLUTIONS%20FINAL(1).pdf; Latin American Commission on Drugs and Democracy, "Drugs and Democracy: Toward a Paradigm Shift," April 2009.

[19] In support of current prohibitionist policies, see "Drug Legalization Would Be 'Catastrophe', Says Ex-White House Drug Spokesman Bob Weiner; Drugs Have Not 'Won the War'; Op-ed Letter in New York Times Today," PR Newswire, June 18, 2009; Bob Weiner, "Time to End Prohibition for Drugs?" *New York Times*, op-ed, June 18, 2009; "How to Stop the Drug Wars," *The Economist*, March 5, 2009; John P. Walters, "Drug Legalization Isn't the Answer," *Wall Street Journal*, op-ed, March 6, 2009.

[20] See for example H.R. 2134, Western Hemisphere Drug Policy Commission Act of 2009; Rafael Pardo and Juan Gabriel Aires, "Before Washington Ramps Up Yet another Losing War on Drugs, Why Not Let A Commission Construct a Better Policy," *Christian Science Monitor*, op-ed, August 11, 2009; Nicholas D. Kristof, "Drugs Won the War," *New York Times*, op-ed, June 14, 2009.

[21] International Narcotics Control Board (INCB), 2010 Annual Report, 2011.

[22] Richard Nixon, "Remarks about an Intensified Program for Drug Abuse Prevention and Control," June 17, 1971. Briefing transcript at John T. Woolley and Gerhard Peters, *The American Presidency Project*, at http://www.presidency.ucsb.edu/WS/?pid=3047.

[23] Ronald Reagan, *National Security Decision Directive 221*, "Narcotics and National Security," April 8, 1986, partially declassified on November 7, 1995, redacted version available at http://www.fas.org/irp/offdocs/nsdd/nsdd-221.htm.

[24] See CRS Report R41535, *Reauthorizing the Office of National Drug Control Policy: Issues for Consideration*, by Kristin M. Finklea.

[25] This requirement was first established by Section 706 of the Office of National Drug Control Policy Reauthorization Act of 1998 (Division C, Title VII, P.L. 105-277; 21 U.S.C. 1705) and has been subsequently amended.

[26] Office of National Drug Control Policy, 2010 National Drug Control Strategy, p. 3.

[27] See specifically Section 489 of the Foreign Assistance Act of 1961 (FAA), as amended, and Chapter 8 of the FAA generally.

[28] According to the 2011 INCSR, 7 provinces in Afghanistan currently cultivate opium poppy, compared to 21 provinces in 2005.

[29] *2011 INCSR*, p. 15.

[30] See CRS Report RL32250, *Colombia: Issues for Congress*, by June S. Beittel.

[31] The first appropriations legislation for Plan Colombia was located in the Military Construction Appropriations Act, 2001 (P.L. 106-246, Title III, Chapters 1 and 2).

[32] In FY2005, ACI funds were also used for counternarcotics assistance in Guatemala and Nicaragua. Currently, ACI funds are no longer used for counternarcotics assistance in Venezuela.

[33] Office of National Drug Control Policy, Drug Control Budget: FY2012 Funding Highlights, February 2011, p. 11.

[34] The Mérida Initiative is named for the city where it was first conceived by Presidents George W. Bush and Felipe Calderon in March 2007.

[35] See CRS Report R41349, *U.S.-Mexican Security Cooperation: the Mérida Initiative and Beyond*, by Clare Ribando Seelke and Kristin M. Finklea, and CRS Report RL32724, *Mexico-U.S. Relations: Issues for Congress*, by Clare Ribando Seelke.

[36] U.S. domestic commitments will be or have already been implemented under the *National Southwest Border Counternarcotics Strategy*, the *National Drug Control Strategy*, the *Security Cooperation Initiative*, and the *Southwest Border Initiative*. See CRS Report

RL33106, *Border Security and the Southwest Border: Background, Legislation, and Issues*, coordinated by Lisa M. Seghetti.

[37] U.S. Department of State, "Mexico: Evolution of the Mérida Initiative," document provided to CRS in January 2010.

[38] *INCSR 2010.*

[39] Office of National Drug Control Policy, Drug Control Budget: FY2012 Funding Highlights, February 2011, p. 11.

[40] Office of National Drug Control Policy, Drug Control Budget: FY2012 Funding Highlights, February 2011, p. 11.

[41] Ibid.

[42] *INCSR 2010.*

[43] U.S. Department of State, Bureau of Public Affairs, "The Central American Regional Security Initiative: A Shared Partnership," *Fact Sheet*, August 5, 2010.

[44] U.S. Department of State, Bureau of International Narcotics and Law Enforcement Affairs, "FY2011 Program and Budget Guide," pp. 182-186.

[45] Richard C. Holbrooke, "Holbrooke's Briefing on Trip to Pakistan, Afghanistan, and Brussels, July 2009," July 29, 2009. For further information on U.S. drug policy in Afghanistan, see CRS Report RL32686, *Afghanistan: Narcotics and U.S. Policy*, by Christopher M. Blanchard.

[46] U.S. Department of State, Office of the Special Representative for Afghanistan and Pakistan, "Afghanistan and Pakistan Regional Stabilization Strategy," January 2010, http://www.state.gov/documents/organization/135728.pdf.

[47] Subsumed under the Illicit Finance Task Force includes a U.S.-Russia Counternarcotics/Financial Intelligence Working Group with the first meeting convened in Moscow in December 2009.

[48] U.S. Department of State, Bureau for South and Central Asian Affairs, *U.S. Counternarcotics Strategy for Afghanistan*, March 24, 2010.

[49] Office of National Drug Control Policy, Drug Control Budget: FY2012 Funding Highlights, February 2011, p. 11.

[50] See CRS Report R40838, *Illegal Drug Trade in Africa: Trends and U.S. Policy*, by Liana Sun Wyler and Nicolas Cook.

[51] Office on National Drug Control Policy (ONDCP), National Drug Control Budget, FY2012 Funding Highlights, February 2011.

[52] The additional agencies and programs include U.S. Forest Service; Court Services and Offender Supervision Agency for the District of Columbia; Defense Department Counterdrug OPTEMPO; Federal Judiciary; Centers for Medicare and Medicaid Services; Health Resources and Services Administration; National Institute on Alcohol Abuse and Alcoholism; Customs and Border Protection's (CBP) Border Security Fencing, Infrastructure, and Technology; Federal Law Enforcement Training Center; Federal Emergency Management Agency (Operation Stonegarden); Bureau of Land Management; National Park Service; Asset Forfeiture Fund; Bureau of Prisons (Corrections Costs); Criminal Division; Office of Federal Detention Trustee; U.S. Attorneys; U.S. Marshals Service; and Federal Aviation Administration.

[53] Office on National Drug Control Policy (ONDCP), National Drug Control Budget, FY2012 Funding Highlights, February 2011.

[54] State Department response to CRS request, February 26, 2010.

[55] U.S. Department of State, *2008 INCSR*, at http://www.state.gov/p/inl/rls/nrcrpt/2008/.

[56] Kevin J. Riley, *Snow Job? The War Against International Cocaine Trafficking* (New Brunswick, NJ: Transaction Publishers, 1996), p. 112.

[57] Colombia is currently the only country that conducts regular aerial spraying of coca and opium poppy.

[58] For further discussion of eradication policy in Colombia, see CRS Report RL33163, *Drug Crop Eradication and Alternative Development in the Andes*, by Connie Veillette and Carolina Navarrete-Frias.

[59] Barnett R. Rubin and Alexandra Guaqueta, *Fighting Drugs and Building Peace: Towards Policy Coherence between Counter-Narcotics and Peace Building*, Dialogue on Globalization, Occasional Paper No. 37, November 2007.

[60] Thom Shanker and Elisabeth Bumiller, "U.S. Shifts Afghan Narcotics Strategy," *New York Times*, July 23, 2009; Staff of Senator John F. Kennedy, "Afghanistan's Narco War: Breaking the Link between Drug Traffickers and Insurgents," A Report to the Senate Committee on Foreign Relations, August 10, 2009.

[61] Ibid.

[62] For further discussion, see CRS Report RL32250, *Colombia: Issues for Congress*, by June S. Beittel, and CRS Report RS21049, *Latin America: Terrorism Issues*, by Mark P. Sullivan.

[63] "Colombia: U.S. Hostages Spotted," *New York Times*, June 10, 2008; "Betancourt, U.S. Contractors Rescued from FARC," *CNN.com*, July 3, 2008.

[64] See, for example, UNODC, Alternative Development: A Global Thematic Evaluation, Final Synthesis Report, 2005, at http://www.unodc.org/pdf/Alternative_Development_Evaluation_Dec-05.pdf.

[65] See, for example, "A Failed Balance: Alternative Development and Eradication," Transnational Institute, Drugs and Conflict Debate Paper 4, March 2002.

[66] See, for example, UNODC, The Economic Viability of Alternative Development, UNODC internal paper, 1999, at http://www.unodc.org/pdf/Alternative%20Development/EconomicViability_AD.pdf; UNODC, Alternative Development: A Global Thematic Evaluation, Final Synthesis Report, 2005; and UNODC, World Drug Report, Chapter 3: Alternative Development, 2000, p. 152.

[67] U.S. Department of Justice (DOJ), National Drug Intelligence Center (NDIC), National Drug Threat Assessment 2008, October 2007, Product No. 2007-Q0317-003, at http://www.usdoj.gov/ndic/pubs25/25921/index.htm#Top.

[68] Statement of the Honorable Michele M. Leonhart, Acting Administrator, Drug Enforcement Administration (DEA), House Committee on Appropriations, Subcommittee on Commerce, Justice, Science and Related Agencies, March 12, 2008, at http://www.usdoj.gov/dea/pubs/cngrtest/ct031208.html.

[69] The INCB is an independent and quasi-judicial control organ monitoring the implementation of the United Nations drug control conventions.

[70] See also James Risen, "U.S. to Hunt Down Afghan Drug Lords Tied to Taliban," *New York Times*, August 10, 2009; "U.S. Drug Agents Target Afghan Poppy Pushers," National Public Radio, July 29, 2009.

[71] U.S. Department of State, Bureau for International Narcotics and Law Enforcement Affairs, Program and Budget Guide, Fiscal Year 2008 Budget, Publication No. 11453, September 2007, p. 92.

[72] U.S. Government Accountability Office (GAO), *Drug Control: Agencies Need to Plan for Likely Decline in Drug Interdiction Assets and Develop Better Performance Measures for Transit Zone Operations*, GAO-06-200, November 2005.

[73] See CRS Report R41576, *Mexico's Drug Trafficking Organizations: Source and Scope of the Rising Violence*, by June S. Beittel.

[74] http://www.state.gov/p/inl/narc/rewards/c27667.htm.

[75] U.S. Department of State, *2008 INCSR*; see also CRS Report RL32724, *Mexico-U.S. Relations: Issues for Congress*, by Clare Ribando Seelke.

[76] Title VIII, International Narcotics Trafficking, of P.L. 106-120, the Intelligence Authorization Act for Fiscal Year 2000 (21 U.S.C. 1901-1908; 8 U.S.C. 1182).

[77] The law was reportedly modeled on Treasury's sanctions program pursuant to Executive Order 12978 (October 1995) against Colombia drug cartels under authority of the International

Emergency Economic Powers Act (Title II of P.L. 95-223; 50 U.S.C. 1701 et seq.) and the National Emergencies Act (P.L. 94-412; 50 U.S.C. 1601 et seq.).

[78] Section 311 of the International Money Laundering Abatement and Financial Anti-Terrorism Act of 2001 (Title III, Subtitle A of P.L. 107-56, the USA PATRIOT Act of 2001) amends the Bank Secrecy Act of 1970 at 31 U.S.C. 5318A.

[79] U.S. Department of the Treasury, Office of Foreign Assets Control, *Impact Report: Economic Sanctions against Colombian Drug Cartels*, March 2007.

[80] See, for example, Douglas N. Greenburg, John Roth, and Katherine A. Sawyer, "Special Measures under Section 311 of the USA PATRIOT Act," *The Review of Banking and Financial Services*, vol. 23, no. 6, June 2007.

[81] See also CRS Report RL33885, *North Korean Crime-for-Profit Activities*, by Liana Sun Wyler and Dick K. Nanto.

[82] See for example R. T. Naylor, "Wash-Out: A Critique of Follow-the-Money Methods in Crime Control Policy," *Crime, Law, and Social Change*, vol. 32, 1999, pp. 1-57.

[83] U.S. Department of State, *2008 INCSR*, Vol. 2, at http://www.state.gov/p/inl/rls/nrcrpt/2008/vol2/.

[84] U.S. Department of State, *2008 INCSR*.

[85] Statement of Dr. Roy S. Godson, Emeritus Professor, Government, Georgetown University, President, National Strategy Information Center, House Foreign Affairs Committee, Subcommittee on the Western Hemisphere, "Violence in Central America," June 26, 2007.

[86] Since 1992, Congress has required that the President submit annual reports that identify major drug transit and major drug producing countries, known as the "drug majors." Major illicit drug producing countries are defined by section 481(e)(2) of the Foreign Assistance Act of 1961 (22 U.S.C. 2291(e)(2)) as a country in which (1) 1,000 hectares or more of illicit opium poppy is cultivated or harvested during a year, (2) 1,000 hectares or more of illicit coca is cultivated or harvested during a year, or (3) 5,000 hectares or more of illicit cannabis is cultivated or harvested during a year, unless the President determines that such illicit cannabis production does not significantly affect the United States. Major drug-transit countries are defined by section 481(e)(5) of the Foreign Assistance Act of 1961 (22 U.S.C. 2291(e)(5)) as a country (1) that is a significant direct source of illicit narcotic or psychotropic drugs or other controlled substances significantly affecting the United States, or (2) through which are transported such drugs or substances.

[87] Barack Obama, Presidential Determination No. 2010-16, "Memorandum to the Secretary of State: Major Drug Transit or Major Illicit Drug Producing Countries for Fiscal Year 2011," September 16, 2010.

[88] See, for example, U.S. Department of State, 1996 International Narcotics Control Strategy Report (INCSR), 2007, at http://www.state.gov/www/global/narcotics_law/1996_narc_report/exesum96.html.

[89] See, for example, Antonio Regalado, "Bolivia Plants Coca and Cocaine Flows," *Wall Street Journal*, August 18, 2009; Office of the U.S. Trade Representative, "Fourth Report to the Congress on the Operation of the Andean Trade Preference Act as Amended," April 30, 2009.

[90] For additional information on the OAS/CICAD Multilateral Evaluation Mechanism (MEM), see the *2011 INCSR*.

[91] Aid subject to withholding included all aid under Chapter 32 of Title 22 of the U.S. Code except (1) aid under Part VIII (International Narcotics Control) of Subchapter I of Chapter 32 of Title 22 of the U.S. Code; (2) any other narcotics-related aid under Subchapter I of Chapter 32 of Title 22 of the U.S. Code; and (3) aid involving disaster relief, refugees, and provisions of food and medicine.

[92] H.Rept. 108-167, Part I, p. 18.

[93] Section 722 of Title VII of USA PATRIOT Improvement and Reauthorization Act of 2005 (P.L. 109-177; 21 U.S.C. 801 note) amended the Foreign Assistance Act of 1961 at Sections 489 and 490; for further explanation, see also H.Rept. 109-133.

[94] As with the drug majors certification process, the President can waive the foreign assistance restrictions if he determines that providing aid to the country is vital to U.S. national interest.

[95] For FY2006, see the 2006 Foreign Operations Appropriations Act, P.L. 109-102; for FY2007, see the Revised Continuing Appropriations Resolution, 2007, P.L. 110-5; for FY2008, see the FY2008 Consolidated Appropriations Act, P.L. 110-161; and for FY2009, see the Omnibus Appropriations Act, 2009, P.L. 111-8.

[96] See CRS Report RL32686, *Afghanistan: Narcotics and U.S. Policy*, by Christopher M. Blanchard, for additional information on this congressional certification requirement.

[97] Ginger Thompson and Marc Lacey, "Mexico Drug Fight Fuels Complaints," *New York Times*, August 19, 2009.

[98] See CRS Report RS22548, *ATPA Renewal: Background and Issues*, by M. Angeles Villarreal.

[99] Current law on the ATPA and ATPDEA is codified at 19 USC 3201 through 19 USC 3206.

[100] The section of the ATPA/ATPDEA, as amended, which specifies the eligibility requirements, currently refers to a section in law – Section 481(h)(2)(A) of the Foreign Assistance Act of 1961 (FAA) – that was subsequently moved to 490 of the FAA. This provision defines successful foreign cooperation on drug control as whether "during the previous year the country has cooperated fully with the United States, or has taken adequate steps on its own, to achieve full compliance with the goals and objectives established by the United Nations Convention Against Illicit Traffic in Narcotic Drugs and Psychotropic Substances...."

Section 490 of the FAA thus establishes a high threshold for drug control cooperation—full cooperation with the United States and full compliance with U.N. standards—that prior Administrations have argued is difficult to prove. As a result, Congress enacted an *alternative* standard for defining foreign cooperation on drug control at Section 5 of the International Narcotics Control Act of 1992 (P.L. 102-583). This provision defines *failed* foreign cooperation on drug control as whether a country has "failed demonstrably, during the previous 12 months, to make substantial efforts—(i) to adhere to its obligations under international counternarcotics agreements; and (ii) to take counternarcotics measures set forth in section 489(a)(1) of the Foreign Assistance Act of 1961...."

Notably, Administrations have used the latter criteria for measuring drug control cooperation, Section 5 of the International Narcotics Control Act of 1992 (P.L. 102-583), for determining whether a country under the ATPA/ATPDEA remains eligible for beneficiary status.

[101] 19 U.S.C. 3204.

[102] U.S. International Trade Commission, *Andean Trade Preference Act: Impact on U.S. Industries and Consumers and on Drug Crop Eradication and Crop Substitution, 2009*, 14th Report, Investigation No. 322-352, USITC Publication No. 4188 (September 2010).

[103] "The International War on Drugs," Cato Handbook for Congress, 2003, 2009.

[104] UNODC, *World Drug Report*, 2008 edition for the stability of drug use patterns and the 2009 edition for cultivation and seizures trends in 2008.

[105] UN General Assembly, Political Declaration, A/RES/S-20/2, October 21, 1998.

[106] UN Commission on Drugs, Report on the 52nd Session, Political Declaration, E/2009/28, E/CN.7/2009/12 (2009).

CHAPTER SOURCES

Chapter 1 – This is an edited, reformatted and augmented version of United States Department of Justice National Drug Intelligence Center Product No. 2010-Q0317-001, dated February 2010.

Chapter 2 – This is an edited, reformatted and augmented version of Congressional Research Service Report RL34543, dated March 21, 2011.

INDEX

#

20th century, 100

A

abuse, vii, 2, 3, 4, 6, 7, 8, 10, 12, 39, 53, 54, 55, 57, 63, 80
Afghanistan, vii, viii, 22, 41, 89, 94, 95, 97, 99, 102, 103, 104, 109, 115, 116, 118, 119, 121, 123, 125, 134, 137, 138, 143, 144, 145, 146, 148
Africa, 42, 44, 93, 98, 110, 112, 116, 145
agencies, 3, 4, 14, 15, 39, 51, 54, 66, 67, 80, 81, 86, 101, 111, 114, 118, 121, 122, 126, 128, 141, 142, 145
agranulocytosis, 6
airports, 33, 97
alcohol abuse, 86
alcohol dependence, 86
Alcohol, Tobacco, Firearms and Explosives (ATF), 3, 22, 83
alien smuggling, 20, 21, 22
amphetamines, 7
Appropriations Act, 132, 144, 148
Argentina, 123, 133
armed conflict, 104
Armenia, 115
arrest, 5, 8, 58, 108, 125
Arrestee Drug Abuse Monitoring (ADAM), 9, 85
arrests, 8, 18, 64, 68, 80, 86, 122

Asia, 32, 42, 93, 94, 95, 100, 120, 128
assessment, 55, 80, 86, 87, 97
assets, 54, 108, 123, 125, 128
authorities, 19, 32, 58, 61, 90, 101, 111, 114, 126, 128
authority, 45, 96, 108, 109, 146

B

Bank Secrecy Act, 147
banking, 61, 62, 88, 128
banks, 61, 62, 63, 87, 88
bilateral aid, 133
biodegradable materials, 11
Bolivia, 38, 91, 104, 115, 116, 119, 123, 131, 135, 140, 147
border crossing, 106
Border Patrol, 21, 82, 86
Brazil, 104, 123, 133
bribes, 125
Bureau of Land Management, 145
Burma, 94, 126, 131, 138

C

cannabis, 10, 11, 28, 46, 48, 50, 51, 87, 95, 129, 136, 147
Caribbean, 12, 15, 29, 30, 32, 74, 83, 93, 102, 103, 104, 107, 121, 122, 123
cartel, 13, 18, 20, 21, 25, 38, 143
cash, 3, 57, 58, 59, 60, 63, 64, 65, 87, 106, 122, 128

category a, 92
Caucasus, 92
Central America Regional Security
    Initiative (CARSI), 104, 105, 107, 108
Central Asia, 92, 112, 116, 145
Central Europe, 93
Chile, 133
China, 44, 64, 133
CIA, 142
Coast Guard, 82, 122, 142
cocaine, vii, 1, 2, 4, 5, 6, 7, 9, 12, 15, 17, 18,
    23, 24, 25, 26, 28, 29, 30, 32, 33, 35, 37,
    38, 51, 68, 89, 90, 91, 93, 94, 95, 96, 98,
    104, 110, 117, 118, 121, 122
cocaine abuse, 6
Colombia, 2, 25, 32, 38, 68, 91, 94, 97, 98,
    103, 104, 105, 115, 116, 117, 118, 119,
    123, 125, 135, 139, 140, 143, 144, 145,
    146
Commonwealth of Independent States, 92
community support, 105
complex organizations, 13, 96
conflict, 20, 91, 96, 118
Congress, 77, 89, 90, 97, 101, 103, 104,
    107, 114, 115, 116, 117, 126, 127, 129,
    130, 132, 133, 134, 136, 144, 146, 147,
    148
Consolidated Appropriations Act, 148
consumption, 94, 95, 102
containers, 30, 32, 104
controlled prescription drug (CPD), vii, 2,
    54
Controlled Substances Act, 66
cooperation, 2, 64, 89, 90, 101, 103, 106,
    107, 108, 117, 122, 125, 126, 131, 134,
    148
corruption, 96, 100, 107, 109, 128, 129, 137
counternarcotics policy, 101, 109, 121, 131,
    137
counterterrorism, 137
crimes, 9, 10, 68, 80, 127
criminal activity, 14, 15, 103, 105, 127, 128
criminal acts, 12
criminal gangs, 4, 15, 67
criminal justice system, vii, 2, 8, 128

criminal violence, 97
criminals, 61, 108, 125
crop(s), 46, 68, 91, 92, 104, 108, 117, 118,
    119, 120, 136, 141, 142
cultivation, 10, 11, 46, 47, 48, 49, 50, 80,
    86, 87, 91, 92, 94, 95, 99, 103, 104, 112,
    118, 120, 136, 142, 148
currency, 18, 60, 64, 87, 88, 107, 127, 128
Customs and Border Protection, 19, 82, 122,
    142, 145

D

Department of Agriculture, 49, 82
Department of Defense, 82, 90, 111, 113,
    115, 116, 121, 128, 137, 141
Department of Health and Human Services,
    7
Department of Homeland Security (DHS),
    82, 142
Department of Justice, v, 1, 77, 83, 108,
    128, 142, 143, 146
depository institutions, 59
detection, 47, 48, 50, 63, 64, 65, 95, 101,
    104, 107, 113, 118, 121, 122
development assistance, 120, 132, 141
development banks, 133
disaster relief, 147
dismantlement, 98
distribution, 3, 4, 12, 13, 15, 16, 17, 31, 32,
    34, 35, 38, 41, 53, 55, 58, 60, 64, 65, 67,
    79, 99, 126
District of Columbia, 9, 145
doctors, 57, 58, 65
DOJ, 67, 142, 146
domestic demand, 108
Dominican Republic, 29, 30, 115, 123
dosage, 14, 52, 87
drug abuse, vii, 2, 4, 7, 10, 54, 65, 80
drug abusers, 10, 54, 65
drug addiction, 8
drug control policies, 131, 136, 137
drug dependence, 6, 10

Drug Enforcement Administration (DEA), 5, 18, 39, 44, 49, 53, 54, 66, 67, 83, 86, 87, 101, 109, 121, 122, 142, 143, 146
drug flow, 34, 101, 109, 122
drug offense, 8
drug smuggling, 18, 19, 21, 29
drug trafficking, vii, 2, 8, 9, 12, 13, 14, 15, 16, 17, 20, 23, 80, 89, 90, 95, 96, 97, 98, 99, 101, 103, 104, 105, 106, 107, 121, 124, 126, 127, 128, 137, 142
drug treatment, 10, 108

E

East Asia, 42, 96, 112, 116
economic assistance, 134
economic development, vii, viii, 89, 91, 95, 137
economic resources, 118
economic systems, 96
ecosystem, 11
ecstasy, 5, 93
ecstasy/MDMA, 5
Ecuador, 104, 115, 119, 123, 135
El Salvador, 115, 123
eligibility criteria, 134
emergency department (ED), vii, 2, 6, 7, 37, 80, 86
enforcement, 4, 12, 13, 19, 22, 31, 32, 39, 48, 50, 55, 60, 61, 66, 67, 68, 80, 96, 103, 114, 118, 122, 142, 143
environmental conditions, 49
environmental impact, vii, 2, 10, 11
Environmental Protection Agency, 11
EST, 110, 112, 113, 114, 116, 119, 124
Eurasia, 95, 112, 116
Europe, 2, 25, 32, 38, 44, 93, 95, 98, 110, 112, 116
Executive Order, 146
expertise, 122
external influences, 120
extradition, 125, 126

F

FAA, 112, 129, 144, 148
farmers, 91, 97, 105, 117, 118, 119, 120, 136, 141
farming techniques, 120
federal agency, 113, 121
Federal Bureau of Investigation (FBI), 8, 58, 84, 142
Federal Emergency Management Agency, 145
federal facilities, 5, 10
federal government, 106
federal law, 19, 68, 79, 142
Federal Register, 135
Field Intelligence Officers (FIOs), 80, 81
financial, 9, 59, 60, 62, 63, 64, 87, 88, 103, 108, 109, 126, 127, 128, 137, 142
financial crimes, 103, 127, 128
Financial Crimes Enforcement Network, 127
financial institutions, 59, 60, 62, 87, 126, 127
financial resources, 9
financial system, 62, 63, 88, 126
firearms, 18, 22, 86
foreign aid, 99, 104, 111, 112, 134
foreign assistance, 90, 101, 104, 111, 114, 119, 129, 130, 133, 141, 148
foreign person, 122
foreign policy, 99, 100, 117, 125, 137
free trade, 135
funding, 99, 107, 111, 117, 122
funds, 61, 87, 89, 98, 101, 104, 108, 110, 112, 113, 114, 116, 119, 124, 128, 134, 144

G

gangs, 2, 3, 13, 14, 15, 16, 17, 20, 22, 52, 67, 80, 107
GAO, 122, 146
governments, 96, 101, 103, 107, 108, 126, 128, 130, 131, 137, 142

Guatemala, 92, 94, 108, 115, 116, 123, 144
Gulf Coast, 76, 77, 81
Gulf of Mexico, 121

investments, 19
investors, 56, 57
Iraq, 22, 92, 110, 112, 113, 114, 116, 119,
    123, 124

H

Haiti, 30, 123
hazards, 7, 11
heroin, vii, 1, 3, 4, 6, 7, 12, 14, 15, 23, 24,
    25, 26, 27, 28, 29, 31, 32, 33, 34, 35, 39,
    41, 51, 54, 68, 87, 89, 90, 91, 92, 94, 95,
    103, 104, 117, 121, 122
Heroin Signature Program (HSP), 39, 83
HIV, 95, 143
Honduras, 115, 123
Hong Kong, 60
House, 62, 67, 143, 146, 147
human rights, 106, 134, 137

J

Jamaica, 30, 123
jurisdiction, 125

K

Kazakhstan, 115, 123
kidnapping, 20
kill, 11
Kyrgyzstan, 115

I

illegal aliens, 22
illicit drug use, 4, 5, 8, 10, 118
illicit drugs, vii, 1, 2, 4, 6, 7, 9, 10, 12, 13,
    18, 23, 25, 28, 30, 31, 51, 52, 54, 64, 80,
    96, 97, 98, 100, 106, 117, 133, 143
illicit substances, 80, 95
immigrants, 18, 47, 50
import restrictions, 43
imports, 44, 68
imprisonment, 9
incarceration, 8, 9, 10
individuals, vii, 2, 4, 5, 6, 8, 10, 20, 21, 22,
    46, 54, 57, 65, 95, 125, 126
information sharing, 80
infrastructure, 97, 98, 120
institutions, 59, 87, 105, 106, 128, 129
insurgency, 97, 102, 109
intelligence, vii, 65, 80, 89, 97, 106, 107,
    113, 122, 141, 142
interagency coordination, 122
International Narcotics Control, 85, 99, 100,
    104, 107, 112, 121, 127, 138, 139, 140,
    144, 147, 148

L

Laos, 94, 116, 119, 123, 139
Latin America, vii, viii, 89, 93, 96, 98, 121,
    122, 144, 146
Latinos, 17, 76
llaws, 7, 28, 44, 45, 68
Lebanon, 92
legislation, 67, 88, 90, 104, 134, 136, 144
lending, 62
local government, 67
LSD, 73

M

manufacturing, 87, 94
marijuana, 1, 3, 4, 5, 6, 7, 9, 12, 14, 15, 18,
    19, 23, 24, 25, 26, 28, 29, 30, 32, 33, 35,
    46, 47, 48, 50, 68, 87, 117, 122
medicine, 57, 66, 147
membership, 14
methodology, 49
Mexico, 1, 2, 3, 4, 11, 15, 16, 18, 19, 20, 21,
    22, 23, 24, 25, 28, 30, 35, 38, 39, 40, 41,
    43, 44, 45, 46, 47, 59, 60, 63, 68, 82, 86,
    87, 92, 94, 95, 97, 102, 103, 105, 106,

107, 115, 116, 124, 125, 133, 134, 139, 143, 144, 145, 146, 148
Miami, 9, 12, 29, 33, 35, 83, 85
Middle East, 93
military, 46, 90, 97, 99, 105, 109, 111, 122, 123
milligrams, 41, 87
misuse, 7, 54, 57, 65
money laundering, 13, 59, 61, 62, 63, 96, 100, 107, 108, 126, 127, 128, 136, 137, 141, 142, 143
morphine, 54, 57
Moscow, 145
Mozambique, 124
murder, 20, 21, 143
Myanmar, 94

Obama Administration, 107, 109, 119, 121, 125
Oceania, 93
offenders, 9, 10
Office of National Drug Control Policy (ONDCP), 11, 81, 86, 90, 101, 105, 106, 107, 108, 109, 110, 111, 141, 144, 145
Omnibus Appropriations Act,, 148
operations, 3, 12, 16, 18, 20, 29, 31, 33, 44, 46, 47, 48, 49, 50, 60, 65, 87, 97, 118, 121, 122, 137, 142
opiates, 6, 73, 92, 94
opioids, 3, 4, 9, 41, 53, 54, 56, 57, 65, 68
opportunities, 106, 113
Organization of American States, 100
oversight, 57, 90, 101, 117, 126, 136

N

narcotic(s), 87, 90, 99, 100, 101, 109, 112, 118, 120, 122, 126, 127, 129, 141, 147
National Defense Authorization Act, 114
National Drug Intelligence Center (NDIC), v, 1, 4, 24, 36, 59, 70, 80, 81, 142, 143, 146, 149
National Forest System, 82
National Institutes of Health, 82
National Park Service, 145
National Public Radio, 146
national security, 100, 134
National Survey, 73, 82, 86
Netherlands, 121, 133
New England, 12, 39, 50, 57, 74, 75, 76, 77, 81, 83
NGOs, 98
Nicaragua, 124, 144
Nigeria, 124
North America, 93, 95
North Korea, 128, 147

O

OAS, 100, 131, 147
Obama, 107, 109, 119, 121, 125, 130, 147

P

Pacific, 16, 42, 50, 74, 75, 76, 77, 100, 102, 112, 116, 121
pain management, 57, 58
Pakistan, 22, 41, 94, 109, 115, 116, 119, 124, 145
Panama, 104, 115, 124
Paraguay, 124
parole, 8
PCP, 73
peer review, 131
personal relationship, 15
Peru, 38, 91, 92, 104, 115, 116, 119, 124, 135, 140, 143
pharmaceutical(s), 5, 11, 54, 55, 86, 94
phencyclidine (PCP), 9, 73
POEs, 14, 25, 28, 32, 33, 34, 44, 52, 59, 64
police, 97, 129, 142
political instability, 96
poverty, 95
Prescription Drug Monitoring Program (PDMP), 3, 57
President, 81, 100, 101, 107, 126, 129, 130, 131, 132, 133, 134, 135, 141, 147, 148
principles, 101, 102
prisoners, 8, 9
producers, 10, 44, 95, 118, 130, 131

psychotropic drugs, 129, 147
public health, vii, viii, 39, 80, 89, 95, 98
public safety, 22, 142
Puerto Rico, 9, 29, 31, 82
purity, 1, 14, 35, 37, 39, 41, 42, 80, 86, 94

R

recidivism rate, 9
reform(s), 99, 105, 106, 128, 137
refugees, 147
regional policy, 100
regions of the world, 91
regulations, 59, 63, 79, 126
rehabilitation, 98, 100
RES, 148
resources, 8, 9, 95, 105, 120, 123
response, 18, 25, 29, 41, 50, 101, 110, 112,
    113, 114, 115, 116, 119, 124, 145
restrictions, 43, 44, 45, 68, 126, 133, 148
rewards, 124, 125, 146
risk, 14, 47, 63, 65, 95, 108, 119
routes, 19, 20, 22, 25, 29, 31, 34, 35, 44, 52,
    95, 103, 110, 118, 121, 125
rule of law, 96, 106, 107, 108, 128, 129, 137
rural areas, 60, 67

S

safe haven(s), 96, 126, 137
sanctions, 131, 146
savings, 17, 62
scope, vii, 99, 131
SEA, 42
Secretary of Homeland Security, 142
Secretary of the Treasury, 126
secure communication, 87, 115
security, 13, 48, 65, 95, 97, 98, 103, 105,
    107, 108, 114, 120, 121, 134, 141, 143
security forces, 105
sedatives, 86
seizure, 2, 14, 18, 25, 30, 32, 33, 34, 35, 47,
    48, 50, 51, 52, 59, 61, 65, 68, 86

smuggling, 2, 14, 18, 20, 21, 22, 25, 28, 29,
    30, 31, 32, 33, 34, 38, 44, 46, 51, 52, 59,
    60, 63, 64, 80, 103, 104, 107, 118, 128
social consequences, 98, 118
social development, 104, 137, 141
social fabric, vii, viii, 89, 95
social justice, 107
South America, 12, 22, 25, 27, 28, 30, 32,
    33, 34, 38, 39, 41, 44, 91, 93, 95, 104,
    110, 120, 121, 134
South Asia, 92
South Dakota, 7
South Korea, 133
Southeast Asia, 14, 42, 93, 94, 120
sovereignty, 97, 126
steroids, 86
substance abuse, 6, 7, 8, 54, 80
suicide, 7
synthetic drugs, 90, 94, 95, 121, 136

T

Taiwan, 133
Tajikistan, 115, 124
Taliban, 98, 146
terrorist groups, 97
terrorist organization, 119
terrorists, 19, 96
Thailand, 92, 133
Title I, 144, 147
Title II, 144, 147
Title V, 144, 146, 147
torture, 21, 143
TPA, 134
trade, vii, 12, 63, 80, 89, 90, 95, 97, 98, 99,
    100, 101, 103, 106, 109, 110, 117, 118,
    121, 125, 126, 128, 129, 131, 132, 134,
    135, 136, 141
trade preference, 129, 135
trafficking, vii, 2, 4, 7, 12, 13, 14, 15, 16,
    17, 21, 27, 31, 32, 38, 41, 58, 80, 95, 96,
    97, 98, 99, 100, 104, 105, 106, 107, 110,
    112, 122, 124, 127, 128, 130, 136
tranquilizers, 5, 86
transatlantic flights, 41

transport, 3, 12, 13, 28, 29, 30, 31, 65, 96, 114, 143
transportation, 12, 13, 17, 18, 25, 27, 28, 31, 33, 35, 47, 64, 67, 80, 141, 143
Treasury, 127, 142, 146
treaties, 99
treatment, vii, 2, 6, 8, 10, 41, 58, 68, 80, 87, 95, 98, 100
trial, 125
Trinidad, 124
Trinidad and Tobago, 124
Turkey, 124
Turkmenistan, 115, 124
Turks, 122

U

U.S. Department of Commerce, 82
U.S. Department of the Interior, 49
U.S. Department of the Treasury, 127, 147
U.S. policy, 98, 100, 117, 118, 137
Ukraine, 92
urban areas, 16
USA PATRIOT Act, 59, 147
Uzbekistan, 115

V

vegetation, 11
vehicles, 3, 28, 31, 64, 65, 115, 117
Venezuela, 92, 104, 131, 144
vessels, 18, 28, 29, 30, 31, 104
Vietnam, 92
violence, 18, 20, 21, 22, 25, 38, 90, 97, 106, 107, 124, 137
violent crime, 14
vulnerability, 61, 62, 96

W

waiver, 134
Washington, 12, 49, 66, 67, 82, 84, 85, 144
weapons, 3, 14, 18, 19, 22, 23, 106, 107
weapons of mass destruction, 19
West Africa, 42, 95, 96, 98, 104, 110
White House, 90, 101, 144
World Health Organization, 86